Reveal

Reveal

Let It Go

We create ourselves constantly as we go along

Bhuvana Mandalapu, M.D.

iUniverse, Inc.
Bloomington

REVEAL
LET IT GO

iUniverse books may be ordered through booksellers or by contacting:

iUniverse
1663 Liberty Drive
Bloomington, IN 47403
www.iuniverse.com
1-800-Authors (1-800-288-4677)

ISBN: 978-1-4759-8410-1 (sc)
ISBN: 978-1-4759-8411-8 (hc)
ISBN: 978-1-4759-8412-5 (e)

Library of Congress Control Number: 2013907045

Printed in the United States of America.

iUniverse rev. date: 4/22/2013

A philosophical and motivational approach to achieve
our potential through knowing and practice

Power of precise, balanced nutrition with meditation
is a valuable and sometimes a miraculous gift.

Bhuvana Mandalapu, MD

To individuals and families that tolerate harsh, ignorant, immature, and childish adults for years and still love and care for them. To my friend Raghava and to the well-being of everyone on earth.

Table of Contents

Preface

LIFE MAKES NO EXCEPTIONS. Even famous people suffer like everyone else. They suffer from family issues, personal tragedies, and losses, and many of them suffer from medical, psychiatric, or neurological disorders. They often try different ways of living, different foods, and different dietary habits. Despite their shortcomings, they achieved excellence and fame for themselves, contributed to their families, and gave much to society just by not giving up their goals. Whatever happened in their lives, they were persistent in trying to achieve their goals. Despite their personal shortcomings, they often achieved superior goals.

Gandhi, Buddha, Darwin, Newton, and Steve Jobs are just some examples of this. They achieved their goal and became famous.

Ronald Reagan and Alfred Nobel achieved success but then suffered devastating diseases when they were older.

Thomas Edison tried different life style practices, including diet, to sustain his health, even though medical science was not so advanced in his time.

J. K. Rowling is another example; she endured financial crises, personal loss, grief, and depression, but she still came up with exceptionally creative and brilliant writings.

Laura Hillenbrand is another example. The author of *Seabiscuit* and *Unbroken* has suffered from chronic fatigue syndrome for decades and mostly still remains confined to her home, but she did not give up. On the irony of writing about physical paragons while being so incapacitated herself, she said, "I'm looking for a way out of here. I cannot have it physically, so I'm going to have it intellectually. It was a *beautiful* thing to ride Seabiscuit in my imagination. I write about people at vigorous moments in their lives; it is my way of living vicariously." (wikipedia)

The list of other role models is endless. Some of them changed the world forever by their contributions. They often suffered from personal, financial, and family issues; endured mental and physical troubles; and withstood various social factors against them, yet their priorities were different and they were only focused on their goals. They had disappointments but were not demoralized. They were great because of what they achieved and also because of the adversities that they faced; all the trouble they went through before their success makes them unique in their respective fields.

From time to time, we come across unsung heroes. I recently met one such person called Gloria.

She is in her early fifties and is very active and energetic; she got a flu shot just like anybody else. Same night, she developed double vision. She felt a weakness in her legs the next day and found it difficult to walk. It became so bad that she could no longer walk. She was admitted to a hospital and got even worse; she needed ventilator support, and after a month, she came out of it. She was able to talk and breathe on her own but was totally paralyzed in both legs and arms.

Gloria was diagnosed with Guillain–Barré syndrome (GBS), an illness that affects one person in a million; according to the Centers for Disease Control and Prevention (CDC) after the Flu shot.

Gloria is making progress day by day. She went from a normal working life to being totally paralyzed and bedridden in just one week. This is sad and devastating to imagine even for a second.

I am Gloria's physician, and whenever I go into her room, she is always so positive, optimistic, and motivated. She wants to learn more, and do more and more therapies to help her improve. Moreover there is always a smile on her face. She has a good family and many friends. She thanks everyone all the time for being supportive. She appreciates their presence.

I always see that remarkably positive attitude and a gleam of determination on her face. Her eyes show that she is not going to give up. I feel more motivated each time I visit her.

A Word from the Author

I COME FROM A place that is very close to a twelfth-century Buddhist university. During the summer, we often went there for a picnic. In those days, I was never aware of what was going on. Back in the classroom, we studied Buddha and learned that he was a prince who had become enlightened. I remember one of his sayings we learned in childhood: "Desire is the root cause of suffering."

Ironically, I later attended a medical school named after Buddha's real name: Siddhartha Medical College. We used to walk past a large framed statue of Buddha on the campus, but I never thought about him. It was just another statue to my eyes.

On graduation day, we all received a memento with a sitting Buddha imprinted on it. Still, there was nothing of the real Buddha in me.

I went through many hurdles to become a doctor and have treated and counseled many patients; looking back, I learned that we know only when we can see with the heart. Like Buddha said, "We can comment only when we face what others face and go through the same feelings as others." Only then can we comment on another's actions. The mere presence of information in front of us means nothing. If we do not realize it, use it, or bring it out of ourselves, "just seeing is not knowing."

We all have Buddha within us; just like he said, everybody could become Buddha as long as they look inside of themselves, learn, and improve with practice. Once we are able to look into own mind with practice, we will find freedom and happiness. We can see our mind more transparently, improve, and live better. So please practice without giving up.

About the Book

He is able who thinks he is able.—Buddha

Reveal: Let It Go is about knowing our shortcomings and accepting them by creating harmony between the conscious and subconscious minds. By doing so, we can overcome all our difficulties and reach our potential.

This book is about consistent practice to get there with harmony.

It is about proving that when we consistently practice the basic concepts of "Don't give up" and "Let it go" and "moderation in practice," we will reach our goals.

Finally, *Reveal: Let It Go* is about rebuilding our soul by continuously learning and improving our brain and our mind's capabilities, with the help of consistent but moderate meditation practice and ideal dietary practices.

While modern medical advancements can help, including deep brain stimulation, magnetic stimulation, ultrasound techniques, neuromodulation of the brain, in restoring lost functions of the brain. Meditation and dietary practices also contribute to above along with the pursuit of consistent happiness.

In a day when you do not come across any problems, you can be sure that you are traveling on the wrong path.—Vivekananda

Meditation

The secret formula of happiness is in your heart.
The secret of success is within the treasure chest of your
own troubles.
The path of struggle to make both of them yours is the
ultimate joy.
The key is in moderation.
Ignite it with meditation.
Reinvent yourself.

IF YOU ARE TOTALLY new to meditation, these brief words will
explain this good, better, best, and perfect friend.

Meditation is nothing, but it makes you fix your thoughts on
what you want so that your mind will create an ultimatum to
your brain to prepare well. It will transmit the proper signals
back to your mind and body to help recoup more, faster.

Daily meditation will help you regain previous levels of functionality
as much as possible and provide pleasure and joy to your soul. Your
joy will be reflected in your face, your words, and your acts. That is
the power and purpose of daily meditation practice.

Part i.

Knowing Briefly About Key Slogans and Pearls before We Start

LEARN TO IGNORE THE negative forces; they will leave like unwelcomed visitors.

Strengthen your gains ceaselessly without giving up the practice.

Follow moderation in practice to sustain it forever.

The world will take care of itself and will go through its own cycles of changes; as long as we take care of ourselves, we do not need to worry about the world.

Trust yourself entirely.

Ignite your inner strength and positive attitude.

Cultivate your mind for better results.

In this ongoing process, setbacks are just stepping-stones and blessings in disguise that add to lead to opportunities and success.

Imagine yourself with more positive forces within. See yourself as you want to be, and beyond.

Be the best artist and architect of your own life. Just like Darwin's theory of individual variation, each mind is fresh, and only your mind knows how to reach your goal.

Imagination is more important than knowledge.—Albert Einstein

The only devils in the world are those running in our own hearts [minds]. That is where the battle should be fought [started].—Mahatma Gandhi

Have no fear, but have self-confidence and keep aspiring to higher goals and bigger standards to achieve them one by one.

The greatest danger for most of us is not that our aims are too high, and we miss them but that our aims are too low and we reach them.—Michelangelo

Whose Job Is It?

This is a story of four people named Everybody, Somebody, Anybody, and Nobody. There is an urgent job to be done, and Everybody was asked to do it. Everybody was sure that Somebody would do it. Anybody could have done it, but Nobody did it. Somebody got angry with that because it was Everybody's job. Everybody thought that Anybody could do it. Nobody realized that Everybody would not do it. It ended up that Everybody blamed Somebody, and then Nobody did what Anybody could have done. --- **Anonymous**

So please, let your "body" do the job for yourself; only you can reach your goals, change your life, and give a better life to you and your beloved family.

Do not become obsessed by the idea of "me and mine," but as far as doing good to yourself, there is no Somebody, Anybody, or Everybody; it is only you that will do it for yourself.

Components of Practice

MODERATION

One splendid evening, a father and his five-year-old son went to watch a movie. During the show, the son became hungry and wanted some popcorn. The father bought him some and innocently added too much butter to the popcorn. The son ate the popcorn, and after the show, they went back home. After dinner, they went to bed. After a few hours, the son woke up with stomach cramps. His mother usually took care of him, and she knew that he did not prefer and could not handle a lot of butter on his popcorn. The son continued to vomit and have discomfort. Finally, the day that had been so splendid ended with discomfort and pain for the son and guilt and unhappiness for the father. His innocent mistake of adding too much butter, not knowing the child's tolerance, led to the mishap, just like a car accident that follows a few seconds of negligence or absent-mindedness.

So moderation is the key to avoiding the consequences of making mistakes. Anything in moderation, either food, speech, actions, or responses, will lead to good or excellent results. Practicing moderation in any given activity will deliver consistently successful results.

This also applies to food intake and meditation. Do not remain in extremes, not too tight or too loose; just keep enough tension, stress, and concern, and it will take care of itself well. You will endure tension longer, sustain stress, and preserve concerns by practicing moderation.

READING

> He that loveth books
> Will never want a faithful friend,
> A wholesome counselor,
> A cheerful companion,
> An effectual comforter.
> **—Isaac Barrow**

This is true, and even though there are many other sources available for data, still try to read on a regular basis. Focus on reading about the magnificence of the universe and nature; about the world's magnificent creations; and about the world's great people and how they struggled, went through difficulties, and succeeded without giving up their goals. Humans have progressed from living simple lives to the advancements of today. In the past, we baked bread and wove cloth; today, we make electricity, rockets, satellites, cars, and cell phones. It is so astounding to me how much we have evolved on this earth. We are so lucky to be part of this planet. Finally, we are here to stay happy and make our loved ones happy with our presence, our acts, and our behavior.

Reading can help you appreciate the gift of life that we have; it can also boost your determination.

Remember, famous people did extraordinary things and achieved great goals while suffering from illness and other shortcomings. They ignored those problems and focused on their goals; they used their genius and their minds to create something worthwhile for the whole world, which brought pride to their families and glory to themselves.

Take the time to read on a daily basis. After a while, it will become a part of you. The lives and ideas of famous people will stay with you, and from time to time, that will help you when you are vulnerable. Reading adds a lot of spirit to your heart and motivates you.

So do not allow illness or disease take your mind and willpower away.

Health Is Wealth

It is best to be healthy, but if you have a disease, it is best to deal with it adding your willpower.

Take the best possible medical care. Steve Jobs, who was a genius, refused modern medical care for a while. Medicine is based on advanced sciences; there is nothing wrong in having confidence in it. It is not possible now to treat every disease, but the future looks so bright with gene therapies, stem cell transplants, and other advances. Science has so much to offer to the future generations.

We should do our best to control and rewire our minds and

thoughts; this can defeat illness and keep it subdued. A strong mind can keep disease under control better.

The mind often shows symptoms that are as common as the disease itself. studies have proved that many symptoms are psychological or psychosomatic. If we have will power and gain insight into our problems, we can easily defeat those symptoms and remain disease free.

Be cheerful to yourself and to your family.

Keep up with the practice of meditation to strengthen your mind, fight disease, and keep it away.

Be a pleasure to those around you.

Discover the power inside. Unlock the secret and pursue happiness and success. Do not go back in time; only look forward and see what can change. Do not let your mood and emotions hold you back.

A man who dares to waste one hour of time has not discovered the value of life.—Charles Darwin

The world does not go anywhere by you being different from what you are now.

The world does not change much in a year. A year is not much time in the span of your life, when you are working for a better self, for a permanent change. Darwin's comment about wasting time is right and was in a different context probably. But as long as we know the importance of life, we can spend years practicing for a better life. To achieve balanced feelings with happiness is not a waste. Every minute put into it is worthwhile.

Spending time consciously, with every movement counted, every event memorized, enables you to live in the present, mindfully. Yesterday has gone, and tomorrow is not here, but today, right now, you can be mindful. Capture the moment, mind, and body in one space, and practice to make every step today a sincere and mindful one. Gradually, you will begin to live right "here and now," and the ruminations will slowly fade away.

You will start enjoying every movement you are alive.

I know in my heart that man is good, that what is right will always eventually triumph, and that there is the purpose and worth to each and every life.—Ronald Reagan

After their enlightenment, the Buddha and Confucius lived lives of peace, but they still practiced meditation every day. They not only enjoyed the tranquility of meditation, they reaffirmed the importance of a positive attitude and regularly practiced their values.

Darwin, Newton, and other famous people achieved remarkable discoveries while facing personal tragedies and overcoming depression, attention deficit, social phobias, and anxiety. They focused all their curiosity and positive energy toward a worthwhile goal, and they never gave up on their targets. This type of meditation is little different from Buddhism.

The end results are different yet similar. The Buddha and Confucius produced extensive philosophical and behavioral approaches for a righteous life, whereas Darwin and Newton unraveled the secrets of nature and creation with their goal-oriented research as meditation, and they did this while overcoming personal difficulties.

Steve Jobs and J. K. Rowling are similar to them. They changed their feelings and overcame their sufferings by producing innovations of technology and literature. Their inventions benefited generations; Rowling changed her emotions into creativity, producing characters that thrilled and amazed the whole world.

They went through so much physical discomfort, mental stress, and suffering, even thoughts of suicide, and one succumbed to cancer. Until the last day of his life, Steve Jobs was doing meaningful thinking and working, ignoring his own suffering and the fear of leaving this world.

CHANGE TO SEE AFTER PRACTICE

There are no time guidelines here; remember, Buddha practiced meditation every day until his last moment on earth, despite being enlightened permanently.

You will soon see a change in yourself that is permanent. You will be more mindful during every movement; you will enjoy situations and conversations consciously and mindfully. You will be involved instead of having your mind be somewhere else.

You will be more goal oriented and productive; your quality of life will improve far better than your expectations.

Overall, you will see the change that you always wanted but were never able to achieve in the past. Your new self will emerge for you to keep forever.

The change will be reflected in all aspects of your life. Others will easily see the change and admire it.

You will discover the absolute joy of walking with your child to and from school. You will enjoy every movement that you are with your loved ones. Every movement will be a joy-filled memory. If you are currently doing things with no joy, almost with your mind and thoughts somewhere else, you can improve that with practice. Your patience, presence of mind, and "living now" feelings will improve tremendously.

Look at your family in their beds every night and morning. How serenely they all look, with the impression that you are there and will take care of them. As long as they feel that you are there for them, they have no worries. Their comfort and support is a strong motivation to accomplish things, not only for yourself, but also to make your loved ones happy and proud of you.

Objects in Air

The mind that is not trained, does not practice, and does not maintain its practice is like an object thrown up in the air.

The object will find its way to the ground due to gravity. Similarly, the mind, if it does not practice or seek a positive attitude, happiness, and joy in a righteous way, always drops down toward unhappiness and gloomy, lazy ways due to the natural preference of sad thoughts. But to be happy and positive, you need effort and engagement. If not, your mind will naturally prefer sorrow, bad thoughts, and sad feelings, and it will ruminate over them and make them like the adobe.

An idle brain is the devil's workshop.—H. G. Bohn

FALLING FRUIT

Even people who meditate and reap the rewards of good practice and thoughts can go back to their old ways when circumstances make them vulnerable. Just like ripe fruit falls down to the ground when it is ready to drop, people can fall prey to negative forces and unhealthy attitudes and thoughts, pulling them toward depression, self-abusing behaviors, killing their self-esteem again during the vulnerable states of economic, physical, and social scenarios and peer pressure.

But unexpected physical, behavioral, and mental health issues also do the same, even if you take medication regularly. Sometimes circumstances and surroundings make us so vulnerable that we cannot endure without succumbing to them.

This is the time we need more courage and practice to sustain the gains of our days and years of practice. Steve Jobs and J. K. Rowling are two notable examples who won over their own illness, one over physical illness, and one over depression, financial burdens, and insecurity, which is almost as bad as cancer.

Live more consciously in those vulnerable times. When we are emotional, we lose logic and fall apart, which can make us lonely. Despite hundreds of people and friends around, you may battle with your own thoughts and emotions; you may not be reasonable or sustain the truth. In those particularly vulnerable times, practicing meditation, sustaining what we did so far, and having a positive attitude can only help you go further in the right direction. Even if it is the end of the line, you can cross the line with self-respect and dignity of the soul.

One day, when my son was five years old, he woke up complaining of foot pain. I thought he might have slept in the wrong position, so I applied a topical cream as he watched TV. Before I left for work, I asked him if he was okay.

He said, "Yeah, I feel better, but there's a storm in Bikini Bottom, where SpongeBob lives." Cute, I laughed.

That time has gone for us, and we do not worry about Bikini Bottom and SpongeBob anymore, we have storms in our own mind to clear up, and we have to develop the courage to face them. Your constant meditation practice can help you prepare for the storms from within and from outside.

A friend of mine who is a poet once wrote, "How good it feels just to fly away from every body and every worry, escaping all the struggles and problems, with the sense of peaceful mind all the time."

I met him one day and asked about this philosophy. I asked, "What is the use of flying away from everything. if your same mind carries the same worries?"

He was logical too and took it in a positive way .

There once was a man who had many outbursts of anger. He decided to try to control his anger with meditation. He left the village and stayed alone in the forest, meditating alone. Months passed. He was no longer angry and did not have any outbursts. One day, while he was meditating, a traveler who had lost his way came up to him and asked the way to the village.

He did not get a response, so he asked again, and again there was no answer. When he asked for the third time, the meditating man suddenly opened his eyes and yelled at him with an explosive outburst of anger.

"I am meditating to control my anger," he yelled, "and you came and disturbed me! How dare you? Go and find the way yourself."

How stupid was that? He wanted to get better, and he practiced meditation, but he should not have avoided people. Avoiding is not the answer. Escaping from circumstances, thinking you are going to get better, is not the answer.

You have to find where the battle is; the battle is in your mind. You can fight it by staying in the same circumstances and facing them rather than avoiding them.

This man spoiled everything that he had done for months; he had an easy opportunity to help the other person with joy. He did not help him; he showed his anger and made him unhappy. He lost his temper and totally lost the purpose and intention of his practice. His meditation was not useful. But if he had not given up and continued to face situations and exterminate his anger, with practice, he would have succeeded. That takes lots of practice in the right direction.

Patience is a virtue.

It does not matter how slowly you go, so long as you do not stop.—Confucius

Practice not reacting to other emotions or situations. At least do not react immediately. Even if someone neglects your company, is unhappy with you, dislikes your feelings, and does not interact with you, do not react with similar feelings in return. Let the flying egos fly freely from them, but do not receive them and do not take it personally. Do not reply with another arrow of ego or false ego. Enter the scene with no expectations or anticipation.

Until you know the true purpose of their behavior, and unless you are involved directly in the scenario, there is no reason to analyze another's feelings and attribute those feelings as directed toward you. Let time determine their purpose; just ignoring them will do the job of creating no animosity. It also gives you peace of mind. If you keep thinking about their behavior and feelings toward you, you create unnecessary ripples within yourself. This needs practice. Each day, when come across these conversations or situations, try to respond with a pleasurable expression.

Leave the scene or situation with no feeling to take out of it, if it's not a worthy or positive one.

Buddha said that if someone throws an object toward him and if he does not receive it, it does not belong to him. In the same way, if you hear harsh words from others but you do not react, they do not exist and will not create anger or a grudge.

Buddha used to practice not responding to any problem or conflict or rumor for a full week. This provides enough time to settle the emotional component involved in the problem. The egos will be erased, logic will come back to its place, and it makes the problem return to its actual size rather than be blown up out of proportion in the wrong direction. It will develop itself toward a better solution or resolve itself as if there was no problem in the first place. The problem will vanish by itself slowly. Patience is a virtue, but you must practice a lot of meditation to attain it.

A wise man once said, "I do not have any enemies. If anybody comes across me, I smile. If they speak, I answer; otherwise I leave the event with no feelings to take with me."

A long time ago, there was a remarkably wise demon king. Two brothers fought in a war against this king, and they finally defeated the demon king with the elder brother's arrow. As the king fell on the battleground, the elder brother asked his younger brother to go and ask the demon king for some words of wisdom. The younger brother thought, *What can this demon teach me in his last minute?* But he was not able to speak against his brother's request, so he went to the demon king and asked what his brother told him.

The demon king said, "Slow and steady wins the race, and too late will turn the honey into a poison."

The younger brother was confused and asked the demon king about these contradictory statements. He wondered if he was delirious and not in his senses.

The king explained each statement: "I would have thought carefully regarding losses and gains before I stared this war. A long time ago, I would have done some good to the people who served me, believed in me, and died today in war with me. A long time ago, I would have helped the families of those who died in this battle.

"It is too late for me to do anything; one should be discriminating and careful with using one's ego. As for judging right or wrong, and making decisions, use one's emotions carefully according to circumstances."

At that moment, he died, and the brother went back and told his elder brother that he agreed with the late king's wisdom.

Before we get back into some more realistic thoughts, let us learn some fascinating facts about the brain. I will only present some curious aspects of the brain here; if you are interested in a more detailed explanation, you can find other resources online and in textbooks.

The Brain

DEPRESSION AFFECTS MORE THAN seventeen million Americans each year, or 1 in 6 people. Anxiety is quite common too. The CDC estimates that approximately 1.7 million people sustain traumatic brain injuries annually.

We come across many other neurological and mood disorders on daily basis among our friends and family members including ourselves can be victims too.

BLOOD AND NUTRIENTS IN THE BRAIN

The brain is supplied by two carotid arteries and two major vertebral arteries, which become the basilar artery. Although the brain is only about 2 percent of the total body weight, it receives 15 to 20 percent of the blood supply. Brain cells will die if the blood supply is stopped, so the brain has top priority for blood flow.

Even though other organs need blood, the body will attempt to supply the brain with a constant flow first.

Brain Values

The brain weighs around three pounds (1,250 grams). The brain gives rise to twelve cranial nerves to supply most of the face and head; four of them are dedicated to controlling the eyes and vision. There are two nerves for taste, one for smell, and one for hearing on each side of the brain. The brain can only survive four to six minutes without oxygen before it starts to die.

There are up to ten thousand synapses, or connections for each neuron, in brain. The brain has billions of neurons. The brain has more fat than any other organ in the body. It does not have any pain receptors for itself. Areas of the brain were identified in a number system discovered by the German anatomist Korbinian Brodmann. For example, the main vision center is called area 17. The main hearing centers are called areas 41 and 42.

The brain is not what hurts when we get a headache. The brain knows how to heal headaches and other ailments when we train it to do so. A complicated mechanism triggers a migraine wave; blood vessels in the head dilate temporarily, and their pain receptors cause the feeling of pain.

It is not true that we only use 10 percent of our brain. Each part of the brain has a purpose, and each part helps the other parts, especially damaged areas. This is called plasticity; some parts can even learn the functions of a damaged area of the brain and perform the duties of that area.

The brain itself is a universe. It sits inside the skull and is actually becoming smaller as we evolve. It is unique in structure and function. Just like the universe is so complex with many galaxies, black holes, stars, and planets, the brain itself is complicated.

Just as we are starting to unlock the complex secrets of the universe, science is discovering the secrets of the brain. Many diseases try to overwhelm the brain and disrupt its connections and functions.

Anatomically, the brain has to function every microsecond, without any break, as long as we are alive. Even in sleep, the brain is resting but functioning, cleaning itself with blood supply and reorganizing neuronal pathways; consolidating the memory, chemical and hormonal secretions streamline the brain for when it is time to wake up and functioning, but it never stops working.

The brain is well equipped with plenty of blood supply, which delivers oxygen and nutrients continuously. The brain is the only network with plasticity, even though it cannot regenerate its damaged parts.

The main nutrient the brain needs is glucose; whatever we eat, as far as the brain is concerned, only glucose helps it to function.

There are many chemicals, hormones, and neurotransmitters within the brain, and it does not need outside chemicals, stimulants like caffeine and alcohol, or other abusive substances. It has a tremendous ability to accept any outside substances and can process and function well in most scenarios.

The brain relies on cerebral blood flow to meet its glucose and oxygen needs. As a result, it is highly susceptible to ischemia (a narrowing of the blood vessels), a partially blocked blood vessel, or an acute blood clot, which can reduce or halt blood flow in a specific location. Once blood flow is reduced, neurological symptoms will start; if a part of the brain tissue dies, it will never regenerate.

The brain needs nutrients just like other parts of the body but in different proportions.

Finally, the brain contains our mysterious mind, which is unique to every human.

Brain Structural Controls

A lot of information has come out regarding Albert Einstein's brain. According to a new study led by Florida State University evolutionary anthropologist Dean Falk, "Portions of Einstein's brain have been found to be unlike those of most people and could be related to his extraordinary cognitive abilities."

The researcher said that Einstein's cerebral cortex was extraordinary, based on surface views. She said that the prefrontal cortex, which displayed extraordinary convolutions, helped Einstein's working memory, daydreaming, and imagining scenarios during his experiments with light beams. His parietal lobes were also unusual, and the right and left sides were different from each other. She said that might be responsible for his visuospatial and mathematical skills.

The two halves of the body, which contain similar organs, one on each side, are seldom exactly similar. So there could be a difference in the right side of the face from the left side, right kidney to the left one, right half of the brain to the left half. Those are within the norms, as long as they do not look pathological.

Some brains are abnormal: microcephaly and macrocephaly (brains that are too small and too large), polymicrogyria (too many convolutions, or gyri, even more than Einstein's brain had), and lissencephaly (agyria, which means too few gyri, or failure to develop convolutions because of defective neuronal migration). This is also called smooth brain or pachygyria.

Polymicrogyria is a developmental malformation, with an excessive number of gyri on the surface of the brain. Either the whole surface (generalized) or parts of the surface (focal) can be affected.

The cause can be genetic, viral, or nutritional deficits during gestation. Children born with this disease may suffer from a wide spectrum of problems, from developmental disabilities to severe mental retardation (quite opposite to Einstein), motor dysfunction, speech problems, and epilepsy and seizure issues.

People with lissencephaly also develop small heads, spasticity, seizures, and psychomotor retardation.

People with these diseases may never show a normal IQ. Having too many convolutions was probably not the answer for Einstein's genius. Something extra may have been added to his brain to help his unusual IQ.

Imagine Albert Einstein, that despite having all those convolutions, if did not care about science. His great intelligence probably came from his additional convolutions but his genius along with his curiosity, and hard work helped him consistently. Hopefully, in the future, we will know more about the brain and intelligence; and will also wish by that time, an artificial intelligence may help those with less than ordinary IQ.

Meanwhile, comparisons with brains of creative people like J. K. Rowling, James Cameron, and Steven Spielberg, can be made. Today, valuable imaging studies make it remarkably easy to get all the anatomical information that scientists need.

BRAIN DEPRIVATION

Buddha starved to a skeletal stage and came near to death by depriving his body of food, water, and nutrients. How could he not have any brain damage or dysfunction until the last moment of his eighty-four years of life? He performed well until his last breath, when he slipped into a coma. In those days, nothing was written; he had to remember every sermon, sentence by sentence. He learned them by heart and delivered his sermons in different locations. He always meditated in open areas and caves, even before he became enlightened. His brain was never deprived of oxygen.

Despite depriving his body of nutrients, he probably escaped brain injury from his starvation due to his perfect meditation, which probably retained his brain and memory capabilities and maintained his body in an ultralow metabolic state.

Once we practice meditation and are able to see the results, they will come without effort; we can express what we have on our mind, and our words will reflect that. Our actions will prove that.

Anatomically, the brain is divided into two halves, the right and left hemispheres. They produce different specialized functions and control movements on the opposite side of the body.

Mental abilities are not entirely separated into the left and right hemispheres of the brain. Some mental functions, such as speech and language, are activated by one hemisphere more than the other. If one hemisphere gets damaged at an early age, these functions can often be recovered in the other hemisphere by neuroplasticity. The two hemispheres perform other abilities, such as motor control, memory, and general reasoning, equally.

Right Hemisphere

This side controls sensory and motor functions on the left half of the body. It is also responsible for artistic functions, including creativity, artistic skills, music, and spatial orientation.

Left Hemisphere

This side is responsible for controlling the right half of the body. It is also responsible for spoken language, written language, reasoning, scientific functions, and mathematics.

Both sides share a lot of common functions, working in harmony. The cerebellum coordinates a lot of activities; it wants to know what's happening in all parts of the brain, at all times. Its main function is balance and coordination. When someone is drunk, this is why their balance and walking are affected.

The brain stem controls the vital functions of the heart, the lungs, and the autonomic nervous system. The cerebellum is in the back of the head, whereas the brainstem is between the right and left hemispheres.

There are many specialized parts of the brain, called the nuclei, which are strategic locations that control functions and reveal their dysfunction easily when damaged because of various acquired and genetic causes.

Nerve cells within these areas, based on their functions, secrete different hormones, called neurotransmitters, to help signal the cells and generate responses to coordinate the whole brain activity in a harmonious way.

The anatomically specific areas of the brain and the neurotransmitters play the main role in the process of generation, treatment, and outcome of disease.

Behavioral Aspects

NOW WE WILL CHANGE the subject to the behavioral aspects of the brain.

Psychology as a scholarly study of the mind and behavior dates back to ancient Greece, ancient Egypt, India, and China. Psychology was a branch of philosophy until the 1870s, when it developed as an independent scientific discipline in Germany and the United States. Psychology borders on other fields including physiology, neuroscience, artificial intelligence, sociology, and anthropology, as well as philosophy and other components of the humanities. Today, psychology is defined as "the study of behavior and mental processes."

Psychology as a self-conscious field of experimental study began in Leipzig, Germany, in 1879, when Wilhelm Wundt founded the first laboratory dedicated exclusively to psychological research. Soon after the development of experimental psychology, various kinds of applied psychology appeared. Many cultures throughout history have speculated on the nature of the mind, soul, and spirit. For instance, the Edwin Smith Papyrus contains an early description from ancient Egypt of the brain and some speculations on its functions.

Philosophers from ancient Greece, including Thales (550 BC), through the Romans developed an elaborate theory of what they termed the psyche (from which the first half of "psychology" is derived), as well as other psychological terms: *nous, thumos, logistikon,* and so on. The most influential of these are the accounts of Plato (especially in *The Republic*), Pythagoras, and Aristotle (especially *Peri Psyches,* better known under its Latin title, *De Anima*). Hellenistic philosophers (viz., the Stoics and Epicurians) diverged from the classical Greek tradition in several significant ways, especially in their concern with questions of the physiological basis of the mind. The Roman physician Galen addressed these issues most elaborately and influentially of all.

China had a long history of administering tests of ability as part of its education system. In the sixth century AD, Lin Xie carried out an experiment in which he asked people to draw a square with one hand while at the same time drawing a circle with the other (ostensibly to test people's vulnerability to distraction). Some have claimed that this was the first psychological experiment.(wikipedia)

EXTRAORDINARY PEOPLE WHO SUFFERED FROM MENTAL ILLNESS (WIKIPEDIA)

Winston Churchill (November 30, 1874–January 24, 1965): This British politician told in his own writings of suffering from "black dog," his term for severe and serious depression. Churchill was best known for his leadership of the United Kingdom during World War II. Widely regarded as one of the greatest wartime leaders of the twentieth century, he served as prime minister twice. A noted statesman and orator, Churchill was also an officer in the British army, a historian, a writer, and an artist. He is the only British prime minister to have received the Nobel Prize in literature and was the first person to be made an honorary citizen of the United States.

Leo Tolstoy (September 9, 1828–November 20, 1910): This Russian novelist was equally known for his complicated and paradoxical persona and for his extreme moralistic and ascetic views, which he adopted after a moral crisis and spiritual awakening in the 1870s, after which he also became noted as a moral thinker and social reformer.

His writings influenced Mahatma Gandhi's nonviolent freedom movement. Besides nonviolent resistance, the two men shared a common belief in the merits of vegetarianism, the subject of several of Tolstoy's essays. He likely suffered from severe depression.

Vincent van Gogh (March 30, 1853–July 29, 1890): The work of this Dutch post-impressionist painter, notable for its rough beauty, emotional honesty, and bold color, had a far-reaching influence on twentieth-century art. After years of painful anxiety and frequent bouts of mental illness, he died at thirty-seven from a gunshot wound, generally accepted to be self-inflicted.

Charles Darwin (February 12, 1809–April 19, 1882): This English naturalist established that all species of life descended over time from common ancestors; he proposed the scientific theory that this branching pattern of evolution resulted from a process that he called natural selection, in which the struggle for existence leads to the survival of the fittest.

Darwin published his theory of evolution in his 1859 book, *On the*

Origin of Species, overcoming scientific rejection of earlier concepts of transmutation. By the 1870s, the scientific community and much of the general public had accepted evolution as a fact. In modified form, Darwin's scientific discovery is a unifying theory that explains the diversity of life. Darwin had ten children: two died in infancy, and another child died at the age of ten, which had a devastating effect on her parents. Charles was a devoted father and uncommonly attentive to his children. Whenever they fell ill, he feared that they might have inherited weaknesses from inbreeding due to the close family ties he shared with his wife. He suffered from mysterious ailments that many now believe included panic disorder and agoraphobia.

In 1882, he was diagnosed with angina pectoris, a disease of the heart. At the time of his death, the physicians diagnosed anginal attacks and heart failure.

Charles Dickens (February 7, 1812–June 9, 1870): This English writer and social critic created some of the world's most memorable fictional characters and is generally regarded as the greatest novelist of the Victorian period. During his life, his works enjoyed unprecedented fame, and by the twentieth century, critics and scholars broadly acknowledged his literary genius. His novels and short stories continue to be widely popular. In 1865, while returning from Paris, Dickens was involved in a rail crash; seven carriages of the train plunged off a cast iron bridge that was under repair. The only carriage to remain on the track was the one in which Dickens was traveling.

Although physically unharmed, Dickens never quite recovered from the trauma of the crash, and his normally prolific writing shrank. He also suffered from depression.

Abraham Lincoln (February 12, 1809–April 15, 1865): Lincoln was the sixteenth president of the United States, serving from March 1861 until his assassination (Wikipedia). Lincoln successfully led the United States through its greatest constitutional, military, and moral crisis: the American Civil War. He preserved the Union while ending slavery and promoting economic and financial modernization. Reared in a poor family on the western frontier, Lincoln was mostly self-educated; he became a country lawyer, a Whig party leader, an Illinois state legislator during the 1830s, and a one-term member of the US House of Representatives during the 1840s. He suffered from severe and debilitating bouts of depression; Lincoln once wrote that depression was "a misfortune, not a fault."

Ludwig von Beethoven (December 17, 1770–March 26, 1827): This German composer and pianist was a crucial figure in the transition between the Classical and Romantic eras in Western music. He remains one of the most famous and influential of all composers. His compositions include nine symphonies, five concertos for piano, thirty-two piano sonatas, and sixteen string quartets. He also composed chamber music, choral works (including the celebrated *Missa Solemnis*), and songs.

By the age of twenty-six, Beethoven began to lose his hearing. He suffered from a severe form of tinnitus, a ringing in his ears that made it hard for him to hear the music; he also avoided conversation. The cause of Beethoven's deafness is unknown.

Beethoven's personal life was troubled by his encroaching deafness and irritability brought on by chronic abdominal pain, which led him to contemplate suicide (documented in his *Heiligenstadt Testament*). Beethoven was often irascible. It has been suggested that he suffered from bipolar disorder.

Sir Isaac Newton (December 25, 1642–March 20, 1726): This English physicist, mathematician, astronomer, natural philosopher, alchemist, and theologian has been considered by many to be the greatest scientist who ever lived. He invented calculus and the telescope. In 1687, he described universal gravitation and the three laws of motion, which dominated the scientific view of the physical universe for the next three centuries. Newton showed that the motion of objects on Earth and that of celestial bodies are governed by the same set of natural laws: by demonstrating the consistency between Kepler's laws of planetary motion and his theory of gravitation, he removed the last doubts about heliocentrism and advanced the scientific revolution. His *Principia* is generally considered one of the most important scientific books ever written, both due to its specific physical laws and for its style, which set standards for scientific publications down to the present time. Newton himself often told the story that he was inspired to formulate his theory of gravitation by watching an apple fall from a tree.

Newton was known for great fits of rage and suffered from several nervous breakdowns. Some sources say he had bipolar disorder, while others say he had schizophrenia. He suffered from mood swings with psychotic tendencies, an inability to connect with people, and a tendency to write letters filled with mad delusions.

Michelangelo (March 6, 1475–February 18, 1564): This Italian Renaissance sculptor, painter, architect, poet, and engineer exerted an unparalleled influence on the development of Western art. Despite making few forays beyond the arts, his versatility was of such a high order that he is often considered the archetypal Renaissance man, along with fellow Italian Leonardo Da Vinci.

In his personal life, Michelangelo was abstemious. He told his apprentice, Ascanio Condivi, "However rich I may have been I have always lived like a poor man." Condivi said he was indifferent to food and drink, eating "more out of necessity than of pleasure" and that he "often slept in his clothes and boots." These habits may have made him unpopular. His biographer Paolo Giovio said, "His nature was so rough and uncouth that his domestic habits were incredibly squalid, and deprived posterity of any pupils who might have followed him." He may not have minded, since he was by nature a solitary and melancholy person, a man who "withdrew himself from the company of men."

BEHAVIORAL ASPECTS OF BRAIN AND MOOD

Personalities

Most of the features of individual personality development are established by the age of ten. This is like a three-lap car race. During the first lap, we learn how things start up and how all others are doing. It is fluid, and the individual features of the personality can change really fast. In the second lap, the prominent features of one's personality become established. The final lap establishes dominant personality traits. After the age of thirty, people can still change themselves with constant practice and by analyzing themselves.

Our personalities become fixed by the age of thirty. But some people with childlike personalities show variations within the same day, expressing diverse and mostly harmless, reckless, ignorant personalities of an impulsive nature.

Personality disorders are extremely complex and hard to change or to treat. There are several personality disorders; if you are interested, you can refer to various Internet sources or a textbook for further reading.

Remember, even a midlife crisis does not change your personality. So if a sudden personality change happens, you should undergo a thorough evaluation before coming to any conclusions.

Before we read about behavioral science, we should learn about some extraordinary people who contributed so much to the field of psychiatry (wikipedia).

Philippe Pinel (April 20, 1745–October 25, 1826) was a French physician who was instrumental in the development of a more humane psychological approach to the care of psychiatric patients, referred to today as moral therapy. He also made notable contributions to the classification of mental disorders and has been described by some as "the father of modern psychiatry."

Sigmund Freud (May 6, 1856–September 23, 1939) was an Austrian neurologist who became known as the founding father of psychoanalysis.

Freud's parents were poor, but they ensured his education. Freud chose medicine as a career and qualified as a doctor at the University of Vienna, subsequently undertaking research into cerebral palsy, aphasia, and microscopic anatomy at Vienna General Hospital. This led in turn to a university lectureship in neuropathology, a post he resigned once he decided to go into private practice. On the basis of his clinical practice, Freud developed theories about the unconscious mind and the mechanism of repression; he created psychoanalysis, a clinical method for treating psychopathology through dialogue between a patient and a psychoanalyst. Though psychoanalysis has declined as a therapeutic practice, it inspired the development of many other forms of psychotherapy, some diverging from Freud's original ideas and approach. He also analyzed dreams.

Freud was an early proponent of cocaine as a stimulant and analgesic. He used it himself for depression, migraine, and nasal inflammation during the early 1890s, before giving it up in 1896.

Carl Jung (July 26, 1875–June 6, 1961) was a Swiss psychotherapist and psychiatrist who founded analytical psychology. Jung developed the concepts of extroverted and introverted personalities, archetypes, and the collective unconscious. His work has been influential in psychiatry and in the study of religion, literature, and related fields.

Individuation is the central concept of analytical psychology. Jung considered individuation, the psychological process of integrating the conscious with the unconscious while still maintaining their relative autonomy, to be the central process of human development.

Henry Alexander Murray (May 13, 1893–June 23, 1988) was an American psychologist who taught for over thirty years at Harvard University. In 1930, he was director of the Harvard Psychological Clinic and collaborated with Stanley Cobb to introduce psychoanalysis into the Harvard curriculum. While personality theory in psychology was becoming dominated by the statistics of trait theory, Murray developed a theory of personality called personology, a holistic approach that studied the person at many levels of complexity. Murray was also a codeveloper, with Christiana Morgan, of the Thematic Apperception Test (TAT), which he called "the second best seller that Harvard ever published, second only to the *Harvard Handbook of Music.*"

He developed the concepts of latent needs (those not openly displayed), manifest needs (those observed in people's actions), "press" (external influences on motivation), and "thema": "a pattern of press and need that coalesces around particular interactions." Murray used the term "apperception" to refer to the process of projecting fantasy imagery onto an objective stimulus. Murray died from pneumonia at the age of ninety-five.

Erik Erikson (June 15, 1902–May 12, 1994) was a German-born American developmental psychologist and psychoanalyst known for his theory on psychological development. He also coined the phrase "identity crisis."

Erikson was a student and teacher of arts. While teaching at a private school in Vienna, he became acquainted with Anna Freud, the daughter of Sigmund Freud. Erikson underwent psychoanalysis and the experience made him decide to become an analyst himself. He was trained in psychoanalysis at the Vienna Psychoanalytic Institute and also studied the Montessori method of education, which focused on child development.

Erikson has been described as an "ego psychologist," studying the stages of development. Each of Erikson's stages of psychosocial development is marked by a conflict (trust" and "mistrust," "integrity" and "despair," etc.); successful resolution of each conflict results in a favorable outcome.

These favorable outcomes are sometimes known as "virtues," a term used in the context of Erikson's work as it is applied to medicine, meaning "potencies." Erikson's research suggests that each individual must learn how to hold both extremes of each specific life-stage challenge in tension with one another, not rejecting one end of tension or the other. Only when both extremes are understood can the optimal virtue for that stage surface. Thus, "trust" and "mistrust" must both be understood and accepted, in order for realistic "hope" to emerge as a viable solution at the first stage. Similarly, "integrity" and "despair" must both be understood and embraced, in order for actionable "wisdom" to emerge as a viable solution at the last stage.

Erikson believed that we go through a certain number of stages to reach our full development, theorizing eight stages from birth to death. According to Erikson, the environment in which a child lived was crucial to providing growth, adjustment, a source of self-awareness, and identity.

Meyer Friedman (July 13, 1910–April 27, 2001) was an American cardiologist who developed, with colleague R. H. Rosenman, the concept of "Type A" personality; Type A people are chronically angry and impatient, raising their risk of heart attack. Friedman often characterized himself as a "recovering Type A."

"Type A personality" soon became part of the national vocabulary, shorthand for the sort of driven individual who feels oppressed by time. This is the person who fumes in traffic, barks at sluggish salesclerks, and feels compelled to do several things at once. Friedman and Rosenman opened up a new field of inquiry into the mind-heart connection, still debated today.(wikipedia)

FRIEDMAN'S TREATMENT OF TYPE A

In treatment programs, Friedman used a series of exercises to teach Type As to emulate the mellower, more thoughtful behavior of people with Type B personality. He would ask them to leave their watches home for a day, to drive in the slow lane, to pick the longest line in the grocery store, and to consciously observe and talk to other people. To force Type As to slow down, he prescribed reading Marcel Proust's *Remembrance of Things Past*—all seven volumes. "He encouraged people to read any and all of the classics. He saw it as a way for people to reenergize or strengthen their right brain [the creative side] which he felt atrophied in people with Type A behavior," said Dr. Barton Sparagon, medical director of the Meyer Friedman Institute at San Francisco's Mount Zion Medical Center. Other sessions concentrated just on smiling, because Type As more typically wore a hostile grimace. "Sweetness is not weakness," Friedman would often tell his patients. When he encountered resistance, he quoted Hamlet: "'Assume the virtue even if you have it not,' for its use almost can change the stamp of nature.

"Type A personalities who succeed do so in spite of their impatience and hostility," he said, listing among the more notable Type Bs Winston Churchill, Harry Truman, Gerald Ford, and Jimmy Carter. In his own case, formulating the theory of Type A behavior was just one of many achievements. Friedman contributed important discoveries in the study of gout and cholesterol and helped develop the angiogram.

Friedman suffered an angina attack in 1955 and had the first of two heart attacks ten years later. As a result of this, Friedman attempted to alter his own Type A personality to reduce stress.

BRIEF NOTE ON TYPE B PERSONALITIES

Type B individuals generally live at a lower stress level and typically work steadily, enjoying achievement but not becoming stressed. When faced with competition, they do not mind losing and either enjoy the game or back down. They may be creative and enjoy exploring ideas and concepts. They are often reflective, thinking about the outer and inner worlds. Furthermore, Type B personalities may have a poor sense of time schedule and can be predominately right-brained thinkers.(wikipedia)

Our behavior resembles the action patterns of animals like happiness, fear, and anger with facial expressions: the startle response and smiling. Further, the right and left hemispheres of the brain are separated into multiple lobes, mainly four on each side.

The frontal lobe is responsible for depression, memory, judgment, social interactions, and speech.

The temporal lobes are responsible for memory and speech; this is the main area where seizures come from.

The parietal lobes mainly control motor functioning and processing duties.

The occipital lobes control vision. The brain stem controls the vital autonomic functions of the heart and respiratory control. The thalamus and hypothalamus control pain and sleep, temperature, appetite control, and other functions.

The brain secretes neurotransmitters that assist ideal functioning, include the following:

Dopamine (lack of this hormone can cause Parkinson's disease)

Acetylcholine (deficiency in this neurotransmitter can cause

Alzheimer's, dementia, and myasthenia gravis)

Serotonin (deficiency of this can cause depression)

Norepinephrine (deficiency can cause depression and anxiety)

GABA (deficiency can lead to anxiety and nervousness)

Epinephrine and norepinephrine and corticosteroids are responsible for controlling stress.

Relaxation techniques are highly effective for stress reduction. Anything that can be done to relax without substance abuse should be done; prescription medications can help to cut down cortical levels, which will also help stress.

Memory is not stored in any one particular area in the brain. The hippocampus, temporal lobes, and frontal lobes are considered as memory areas, but it is a function of the brain overall rather than limited to certain brain cells. That is why when brain injuries initially cause memory dysfunction, recovery is possible due to other brain areas increasing memory capabilities.

Remember: The mind and disease also have a bidirectional relationship. Disease affects the mind, and the mind affects the disease.

Defense mechanisms are denial, dissociation, rationalization, reaction formation, regression, repression, sublimation, or suppression. There is no reason to deny unconscious thoughts or regress to a childish state. There is no reason to avoid unacceptable thoughts; we want to face them and clear them away. Sigmund Freud's psychoanalytic theory stated that repression kept the unconscious mind from surfacing into consciousness. If an unconscious aspect affects behavior, the conscious mind does not have access to the unconscious mind. The goal of meditation practice is creating harmony between the unconscious mind and the conscious.

Examples include trail and error, moderation, reinforcement of positive behaviors, and biofeedback. Others techniques include behavioral reconditioning, cognitive restructuring, systemic desensitization and self-control, and self-management techniques.

SUCCESS

Let no feeling of discouragement prey upon you, and in the end you are sure to succeed.—Abraham Lincoln

Opportunity is missed by most people because it is dressed in overalls and looks like work.—Thomas Edison

Success is walking from failure to failure with no loss of enthusiasm.—Winston Churchill

To succeed in life, one should have dedication, determination, and commitment. Remember, an aimless person is a nameless person. Hearts never grow old, but experience grows, expertise matures, but the drive never flags, nor the ambition to see what is ahead and to improve new ideas and new plans of fresh thinking.

People do not live until they begin to discipline themselves; until then, they merely exist.

The predetermined soul will reach its predetermined goal anyway.

But the course of action keeps changing as time goes on and we give our sincere effort to achieve our goals.

Take Steve Jobs as an example. He tried many things and did not stop trying, even while exploring other things.

In the same way, J. K. Rowling is an exceptionally prolific and creative writer. If she remained in her depression, we would not have seen her books. But her predetermined soul did not let that happen. She reached her predetermined goal in the form of Harry Potter. And we do not know yet how much more is going to come from her. What is her predetermined destiny to be?

So that is not the end of it. We do not know what the soul has determined and what is going to be the true predetermined goal and destiny in many cases.

Some people hit the lottery after buying just one ticket, and other people lose with multiple tickets in hand. Still, even if it is a lottery, it is also the predetermined soul reaching its goal and destiny. We can call that karma or fate, but again, it is predetermined.

But our duty is to do the best by choosing our goal based on the current situation. As conditions and opportunities decide, make a sincere effort to achieve that goal. And continue to pick up new ideas and goals and keep living life as it comes.

Naturally, no one can tolerate a life of misery. But by choice, an idle mind may choose to be sad, may prefer to ruminate on its thoughts, may worry, may go back to bad habits and instincts, and may look for laziness, immorality, and sadness. To be sad and down in dumps is the natural preference of the mind.

To be cheerful and happy requires effort. To keep sadness away, we need consistent awareness and conscious effort. To keep off the lingering negative thoughts that are trying to pull the mind toward them, we need constant practice. To avoid its natural tendency toward sadness, we need to work on it on a daily basis.

The predetermined soul will reach its predetermined goal.—Swami Vivekananda

RUMINATION

This is the worst of all. You are driving with your son, but you cannot make any meaningful conversation; you do not even remember that he is in the back seat. You do not enjoy the drive or the surroundings; you do not even observe what is around because you are so involved in your ruminating thoughts. They do not leave until you act firmly and keep them away with practice. The same worry again and again, the same grudge, the same feelings of anger, sadness, despair, go again and again in your mind, giving you a sense of unusual self. How to tackle them is a tough question; only conscious practice to move away each thought will help.

SELFISH/HARSHNESS

Everyone in this world is selfish. Unselfish people, those with no desire, are rare. A lot of us survive on mutual benefits. We help each other on occasions, and the recipient immediately forgets the favor. It is the way of life.

Even if someone did ten favors to someone else, if he expressed harshness or unkindness, he will not be forgiven. All the former favors disappear instantaneously, and only the revolt remains. That is the way the instinctive mind was designed. It remembers only the absolute present favors and forgets even the recent ones. This is exactly the opposite of negative emotions, which will never be forgotten and can develop into grudges. Harshness evokes anger. Buddha said that harsh words will come back to you quickly and so stay only with good words.

So the solution is to not be harsh to others. Do favors with no return expectations. That will alleviate the authority of your subconscious mind to demand, so no disappointments will come. If any unexpected favors come, then accept with joy.

PATIENCE/BOREDOM

In the olden days, we never heard about boredom. With few modes of entertainment, most people spent their time finding their food, preparing food, fetching water, taking care of household animals, and making their daily needs happen. With all that action, the occupied mind did not feel boredom.

During Buddha's time, we never heard of boredom. The only prominent follies were fear, jealousy, violence, laziness, and grudges. Communities were already established by that time. People were able to communicate with each other and discuss things, and entertainment and sports came into existence. Still, everyone had to meet their daily needs, and all that effort consumed most of their daily activity. Some people spent time in meditation and spiritual practices.

Buddha himself scheduled his time; he regularly meditated for two hours and walked in the evening; he also preached, meditated, and slept. How masterly was he to do that for forty years?

Like in Hermann Hesse's *Siddhartha*, he was able to wait, write, or counsel and fast with daily meals, free of frustration, anger, and boredom.

Here is a story from Vivekananda: There once was a veritable sage who taught his son everything that he knew; he wanted him to learn everything else he had to know that he could not teach him. So he asked his son to go and see the king, who was well known for his holiness, to learn whatever he could from the king. The son traveled many days through the forest; when he reached the castle door, he informed the guards, who told him to rest in the waiting hall while they informed the king about his arrival. The whole day passed but the king did not come. After three days, still there was no trace of the king. The sage's son never came out of the room. At dusk on the third day, the king came to the waiting hall and saw the sage's son, sitting in meditation. He had no food, other than some water, in three days. He greeted the king with a pleasant face and said that his father had wanted him to learn what he could from him. The king said, "I do not know what your father taught you or how you learned, but there is nothing else you need to learn, especially from me. You can go back and tell your father about my comments." The sage's son's face was pleasant, even after waiting for three days to meet the king. He had no hunger-induced anger, frustration, or exhaustion after all that travel.

But today, we complain, even with plenty of entertainment in all forms: music, cell phones, vibrant surroundings, and shops. We feel this new phenomenon of boredom or impatience. This was something I learned a few years ago while talking to my boss about his career.

He told me that he and his wife were both busy in their practice, and they had three children to care for. Two went to daycare, and the third one sometimes came to the clinic, crawling around the office. When I asked how they spent time with kids, he said, "It was up to us how much time we wanted to spend with them; for them, time goes on and the day passes any way in their own world. They do not know about boredom." I realized that boredom was an adult phenomenon; innocent children lived life without any worries, surrounding influences, or mental torture.

The daily meditation that we do with our activities can be done while waiting Either you are in a comfortable chair or standing in the line just try to calm your mind and stand still or sit down quietly with peace of mind until your turn comes. That joy is uncomparable and unique.

That Is Their Place Too: Moderation

Fear, anger, lack of self confidence, lack of speech control, childishness, jealousy, grudges are the opposites of positive thoughts and wisdom, like yin-yang. They live right inside our mind. That is their place too, just like awake and sleep, joy and sorrow, pain and pleasure. Just like we work hard to perceive pleasure and joy, we need to work hard to suppress or extinguish the negatives within us. We have to keep them in silent mode.

As Needed

"Eat as needed, sleep as needed, spend as needed, talk as needed." These are the most famous words of Buddha in practice.

A smart woman once said to me, "It is not how much you earn, it is how much you save that is crucial."

Excessive eating causes many direct and indirect health issues. Increased metabolic needs leads to metabolic syndrome and increased circulatory demands. The heart has to work more to pump more blood to vital tissues, including to excess fat deposits.

The digestive system will become overburdened and could fall prey to issues like GERD, gall stones, and pancreatitis.

The kidneys have to filter more protein and metabolic wastes, and they may fail in the long run. Increased weight causes back and neck pains, with mobility issues. Sleep needs also increase, and sleep apnea can occur, which in turn causes more health issues.

Normally, a third of our life is spent in sleep, even in highly productive and hard-working people. So we do not want to waste life in further excessive sleep.

So excess eating, other than giving temporary satisfaction to the tongue with taste, will not do any good to anyone. Laziness of the mind or the body is the most common reason for excessive eating. Free time tempts your tongue and vision. That is why most people become couch potatoes and start watching TV and eating. Leisurely watching TV is a potent stimulator of eating. Just like fire and gas combine to make a bigger flame, one provokes the other, and by the time we realize that we have gained weight, it is extremely difficult to shed it.

Moderation with awareness is the key to success. To create a healthy state, increase the longevity of our precious organs, and keep the mind sharp and bright, we need to take control over excessive eating, sleeping, and talking. With organ transplant and artificial organs, we may live longer, but not without consequences. The immunosuppressants that are used in organ transplants is intolerable to other healthy parts of the body. Why should we lose something in the first place to get something else? We should prepare better to keep our bodies fit.

This also applies to wealth. Save for a rainy day. Your body gets habituated to luxuries and will keep asking for them. Your uncontrolled mind listens to that and will not work for the common good anymore. Teach moderation in every aspect of the life, especially spending. Only practice can help you eliminate the excess.

Depression

No one is exempt from depression. Not everyone goes into clinical depression that needs treatment, but some people develop depression with frequent recurrences. Just like we commit smaller or bigger mistakes, depression may occur in our lives at some point. Whether situational or chronic, we may be able to cope with it or not. The issue is how subtle, chronic, or dysthymic it becomes. Dysthymia is the medical term for chronic, subtle unhappiness; severe depression can last throughout our life too.

Buddha became depressed when he saw the four occurrences

(human suffering including old age, Illness, death). He was depressed and questioned himself about life and existence beyond the palace walls.

He focused on depression and worry by questioning the nature of the mind. He tried to find a cure for all the sufferings of humanity, of which depression is a critical component, whether it is financial, family oriented, health based, or pain related.

During Buddha's time, depression was treated with compassion, philosophy, and attention to the other's needs. This successful approach was the first behavioral therapy.

With the help of modern medications, therapy has expanded to other modalities.

For those who can cope, rebound from depression, and take it as a challenge, Buddha's words are quite enough and still the best treatment.

It may be different for others; current evidence shows genetic biochemical imbalances that can occur in our brain. We have to use a comprehensive approach and deal with depression on a case-by-case basis.

A physician's assessment and antidepressant medications can be quite useful, either for the short term (six to nine months) or longer. There are several types of medications, and each patient may need a different type.

In addition to medication, vagal nerve stimulation can treat medically resistant depression. This involves looping a wire around the vagus nerve, and a pacemaker-like device stimulates the nerve, which can resolve or control depression.

Transcranial magnetic stimulation is another way of treating depression. The brain is stimulated in different parts with magnetic energy.

Biofeedback has been used to develop insight into depression, and meditation is quite useful in conjunction with other modalities. Addressing social issues, avoiding intoxicants, using proper pain control, and treatment of other physical illnesses will help end depression.

Some patients are given electro convulsive therapy (electric shock treatment) as a last resort. Despite every effort, unresolved severe depression often results in suicide, leaving the loved ones behind.

Dreams

There are two types of dreams that occur in sleep(NREM or deep sleep and REM or Active sleep dreams). Dreams can shed light on the working of the human mind. Meanwhile dreams are the keys to success. So Dream (not sleep related) your success and work toward your goal until you fulfill the purpose of the dream.

The dreams that come during sleep sometimes offer a subconscious, cognitive synthesis, resulting in a conscious insight into a tricky problem.

The latest findings indicate that most people dream during the course of six to eight hours of sleep at night.

I'm not talking about people with PTSD or other problems that make scary dreams or nightmares, but many people pay attention to their dreams, not without profit to themselves or to the world.

People with low intelligence sleep better and have fewer dreams. Overall, if you don't dream during sleep, no harm is done.

But we must dream about goals in a positive way and strive to achieve them consistently.

Foggy Brain

Children often have this condition. If no reason is identified, they are often treated for attention deficit disorder (ADD). This is more prevalent in adults, especially people with psychiatric concerns and fibromyalgia. It is not the mild cognitive dysfunction of dementia associated with Alzheimer's. It is a common complaint of people with fibromyalgia, depression, underlying dysthymia, PTSD, poor sleep, insomnia, or other untreated physical ailments. It also happens to people with less exposure to sunlight or a lack of vitamins or other nutrients. Fluctuating blood sugar and blood pressure can cause similar symptoms. It can be chronic and cause an impact on people's lives. Just like pain and fatigue, this is another issue to worry about. People can become obsessed with this and ask themselves why they always feel foggy, sluggish, and gloomy. They do not feel normal.

Foggy Brain Symptoms

One feels like one wants to get an electric shock to the brain to jump-start it. Symptoms of brain fog can range from mild to severe. They frequently vary from day to day, and not everybody has all of them. Symptoms include the following:

- Difficulty recalling known words, use of incorrect words, slower recall of names.

- Forgetfulness or inability to remember what was read or heard.

- Not recognizing familiar surroundings, easily becoming lost, having trouble recalling where things are.

- Inability to pay attention to more than one thing, forgetfulness of the original task when distracted.

- Trouble processing information, easily distracted.

- Difficulty remembering sequences, transposing numbers, trouble remembering numbers.

- Feels gloomy all the time like in a rainy, foggy, cold winter day.

Treatment/Remedies

Treat pain, insomnia, feelings of depression and dysthymia. Increased exposure to sunlight daily. Some people do not come out of the house much. Those who stay indoors suffer from foggy brain more. They can sit in front of a bright light for fifteen to thirty minutes every day in the morning.

Anybody with brain fog should sit in the sun during the middle of the day; exposure to the sun can help get rid of fatigue, some pain, and depression.

Direct exposure to the sun is not a risk in moderation; do it repeatedly ten times each day during the middle of the day. If this is not possible, just sit in the sunlight for thirty to forty-five minutes in the morning.

You should take a daily multivitamin and develop a healthy diet; avoid excess weight, which can also make you feel sluggish and foggy. Drink a good amount of fluids: sugarless, nonstimulating beverages. Some helpful foods are fruits, vegetables, and carbohydrates (but not refined sugars). Fish (omega-3), eggs, canola oil, and other oils are also good. Some people use energy shots, excessive coffee, and stimulants today. Make sure your health condition permits this, and be careful of any side effects with energy drinks. Any stimulants should be discouraged strongly. (Disclaimer:Not everyone will benifit from this advice and readers should consult their doctor before making any dietary changes).

INSOMNIA

Humans spend a third of their life in sleep. While every hour of life is precious, sleep itself is valuable, and every person's sleep needs are different. There are many misconceptions regarding sleep needs and the quality of one's sleep.

After childhood, most of us experience lighter sleep states, and some dream sleep still persists throughout the life. The deep sleep decreases year by year in both quality and quantity. Older people will have some other changes like going to sleep and waking up earlier. They spend most of their sleep in lighter stages and are easily aroused.

Only your doctor can evaluate your sleep and give you the best advice. But insufficient sleep is the most common sleep problem in the United States; more than eighty different sleep disorders have been identified sofar.

Sleep is influenced by many factors, including health problems, physical and mood disorders, environmental issues, medications, financial problems, and personal issues.

People with sleep disorders can become sleepy during the daytime, which will impair their abilities, performance, and productivity; they often do not achieve their optimal goals. Mood disorders, irritability, and unnecessary conflicts are other consequences of poor nighttime sleep.

Psychiatric problems can cause sleep disturbances; sleep difficulties can cause flare-ups of both physical and psychiatric ailments. Sleep difficulties could be with the initiation or continuation of sleep.

Insomnia is a significant public health problem because of the associated risks and consequences. It is difficult to treat insomnia just with medication.

People with insomnia can feel fatigue, malaise, lack of attention, concentration issues, memory difficulties, social problems, vocational dysfunction, poor school performance, irritability, and lack of motivation. They are prone to having accidents at work and while driving. They often get tension headaches, migraines, GI upset, and irritable bowel syndrome due to lack of sleep. This further escalates into concerns or worries about sleep and makes it difficult to initiate and maintain sleep. The lack of restorative sleep leads to further deterioration of physical and mental health.

Sleep difficulties or insomnia can become chronic and lead to many other difficulties. They are numerous, as mentioned above, and can lead to self-medication, such as alcohol abuse. Using over-the-counter or prescription medications can lead to dependence, substance abuse, or worsening of depression. Workplace accidents, absenteeism, and daytime difficulties with performance and cognition can occur. Even suicide is a risk.

As mentioned, medications alone are not the answer. Cognitive and behavioral therapies can help. Optimizing food intake, healthy dietary habits, timing of dietary intake, limiting stimulants, and stopping any stimulant use by the afternoon are also useful. Exposure to the sun in the morning and practicing sleep hygiene (maintaining regular sleep hours)are also effective, as are biofeedback, relaxation stimulus control techniques, and meditation. It also helps to avoid anticipatory anxiety while in bed and ignore the thought of insomnia.

It is particularly helpful to clear up any misconceptions regarding sleep and insomnia. Some people perform well with only brief sleep; you could be a "short sleeper." Many famous people slept remarkably little in their life but still performed well. These facts can clear up some false impressions and expectations regarding your sleep needs.

Normal Sleeper

Most adults have regular sleep needs; they function better with seven to nine hours of sleep, and about two-thirds of Americans regularly get this amount. Children fare better with eight to twelve hours, and elderly people may need only six to seven.

One-third of Americans are sleep-deprived, regularly getting less than seven hours a night, which puts them at higher risk of diabetes, obesity, high blood pressure, and other health problems.

SHORT SLEEPER

Short sleepers are about 1 to 3 percent of the population. They function well on less than six hours of sleep, without feeling tired during the day. They tend to be unusually energetic and outgoing.

SOME FAMOUS SHORT SLEEPERS (WIKIPEDIA)

Leonardo Da Vinci used to take fifteen-minute naps every four hours.

Michelangelo slept four hours per day.

Napoleon Bonaparte (August 15, 1769–May 5, 1821) was a French military and political leader who rose to prominence during the latter stages of the French Revolution and its associated wars in Europe. As Napoleon I, he was emperor of France from 1804 to 1815. Napoleon existed on three or four hours of sleep a night. It was said that he used to take catnaps while riding his horse.

Winston Churchill only spent six hours in bed every night. However, he used to take a complete nap every afternoon for up to two hours.

Thomas Alva Edison slept only three to four hours a night.

Margaret Thatcher (born October 13, 1925) was the longest-serving (1979–1990) prime minister of the United Kingdom in the twentieth century, and the only woman ever to have held the post. She sleeps only four hours a night.

Requirements for sleep vary widely. Most adults need the traditional seven or eight hours of sleep a night, but short sleepers function well on only three or four hours. Many people overestimate the amount of sleep they need and underestimate the amount they actually get during a restless night. However, if loss of sleep impairs a person's ability to function well during the day, it might indicate a problem.

Sleep Disorders

People wake up many times during the five to seven cycles of sleep during the night and then go back to sleep. As long as you feel rested, you need not worry about the lack of sleep.

Lighter stages of sleep are the most common in adults. We sleep mostly in Stage 1 and 2. People often crave for deep sleep and think that they are not sleeping, but they are wrong.

Because we spend most of our time in superficial or light sleep, even minor noises can wake us up, and we are often aware of what is happening around us. But our brain is still resting in lighter sleep modes. Ruminating over the lack of sleep can make you restless the next day, and the tension of anticipating a lack of sleep can become a recurring pattern, leading to insomnia.

Some nights we sleep well, and other nights we do not. As long as we sleep well four to five nights per week we can cope. Some days there will be more, and some days there will be less; even with no sleep, we can still function reasonably well. Taking away the anxiety and worry over sleep will make things better on its own so it does not become an issue.

Despite taking precautions, true insomniacs may need sleep aids or even stronger medications. They should select the right ones that do not cause habituation.

A good night's sleep makes you feel better in the morning. Pain, stress-related headaches, fatigue, and frustration can improve with a refreshing six to eight hours of sleep. This may apply to short sleepers too.

Some sleep problems are related to psychiatric issues or alcohol or substance abuse. Conditions like obstructive sleep apnea, central sleep apnea, restless leg syndrome (RLS), periodic leg movement syndrome (PLMS), and narcolepsy should be properly diagnosed and treated by your physician.

Loud irregular snoring and daytime sleepiness are hallmarks of obstructive sleep apnea. The irresistible urge to move one's legs are features of RLS and PLMS, which can result in non refreshing sleep on a chronic basis. Some problems may need sleep testing before being diagnosed and treated, whereas others can be helped with medications alone.

HISTORICAL FIGURES WITH SLEEP DISORDERS

Throughout history, there have been many extraordinary people who suffered from insomnia. They came from all walks of life and were immensely talented. In spite of their inability to enjoy the benefits of a full night of deep, peaceful, relaxing sleep, these gifted individuals had the strength of character to cope with their sleep problems and achieve extraordinary things in their lifetime.

Sir Isaac Newton was known to have suffered from inability to sleep and also had severe depression. Benjamin Franklin suffered from severe bouts of insomnia. Abraham Lincoln and Theodore Roosevelt also were insomniacs.

Sleep Thoughts of Famous People

Fatigue is the best pillow.—Benjamin Franklin

A good laugh and a long sleep are the best cures in the doctor's book.—Irish proverb

The worst thing in the world is to try to sleep and not be able to.—F. Scott Fitzgerald

It is a common experience that a problem difficult at night is resolved in the morning after the committee of sleep has worked on it.—John Steinbeck

The best bridge between despair and hope is a good night's sleep.—E. Joseph Crossman

Sleep is the best meditation.—Dalai Lama

All these above sayings apply to those called good sleepers or routine sleepers. Short sleepers do not need to worry about the above comments; they do as good as others with small periods of sleep. Evaluate your usual sleep patterns and requirements, fill that time frame regularly, and do as good as any other sleeper as per cognitive and health issues.

INSOMNIA

The short-term prognosis depends on the cause and can be helped by short-term hypnotic agents as needed.

The long-term prognosis depends on multiple factors like maintaining sleep hygiene and avoiding medications that can make one dependent. Overall, insomnia is not a life-threatening problem. It is often caused by underlying medical issues that cannot be fixed quickly with either medicines or devices.

Timing of the Sunlight affects the pineal gland, which secretes melatonin. Melatonin helps us sleep and regulates body temperature (thermoregulation). So maintain routine activities every day. Try to be exposed to sunlight in the morning on a daily basis.

Melatonin rises in the evening until early morning and declines thereafter. Light exposure suppresses the production of melatonin, so late evening light exposure can delay the melatonin surge from pineal gland.

Practicing sleep hygiene is useful even for people without insomnia. Some tips include reducing exposure to sunlight after four o'clock, shutting off the bedroom lights during sleep time, and not eating after eight o'clock (if possible, stop eating as early as four o'clock).

Do not worry about sleep dreams. In active sleep, also called REM sleep, dreams are irrational and complex. Deep sleep dreams, also called non-REM sleep, are simpler and more realistic. If you do not have dreams, there is nothing to worry about. With sleep hygiene and meditation, cognitive performance, learning, and memory all should improve. Reaction time also will improve. People often underestimate the negative impact of sleep deprivation on cognition and performance.

Many individuals sleep less during the week than on weekends. Average sleep is one to two hours less, and younger adults sleep less than seven hours per night on weekdays. Older adults are more resilient to sleep deprivation than young adults. Usually children sleep very well until adolescence; after that, delayed sleep phase problems start due to their activities. With good sleep, vigilance, alertness, and vigor will improve. Tiredness, lethargy, and fatigue all get better. Pain tolerance improves, and seizure thresholds grow; people with epilepsy see fewer seizures. In fact, sleep deprivation is one of the main triggers for breakthrough seizures. Resistance to infection also increases with good sleep.

Sleep Hygiene Techniques and Meditation

If you cannot fall asleep after you practice these sleep hygiene techniques, do meditation in the morning for half an hour to one hour. If you cannot stay asleep and wake up after a few hours, then do meditation both in the morning and evening.

If you cannot sleep after four o'clock in the morning, do not stay in bed. Wake up and go on with your daily morning activities, including meditating.

Wise Man

There are thousands of reasons to worry; a thousand reasons for anxiety can oppress a fool, day after day, but not the wise man.

Even the severed branch grows again, and the sunken one returns. Wise men are not troubled by adversity.

The one serious conviction that a person should have is that nothing is to be taken too seriously; everyone should learn to let go. Luck may sometimes help, but work always helps. If you do not worry about a misfortune for three years, it will become a blessing.

A spirit filled with the truth must direct its actions to the final goal.—Gandhi

Target

Different people in different ways achieve their targets in their life. Everybody should have their own targets and goals. A person without an aim is like someone with no name. How do some people reach their target? It is different for everyone. As long as you reach it eventually, morally you are a winner. Success is defined as winning at the right place and the right time.

Opportunity comes at the right time and right place. Success by definition should make you happy and joyful. As we move relentlessly toward success, we often miss the target several times. It may take many different zigzag ways; we may face obstacles from time to time, but as long as we do not give up the vision of the target and continue to make a conscious effort, we are not a failure.

We may not yet reach the target to have that sense of success. While traveling toward success, do not forget to enjoy and accept the pain as a blessing that your one success will answer all your efforts.

All mistakes and worries can be erased with success. There are positive and negative forces within us. We lose logic when we are emotional. There is nothing to repent. Past is past, and we should only look forward.

A long time ago, there was a young man living with his mother. He was a good and totally innocent man. Every day he did his daily work, went home, and helped his mother in everything. One day, he came across a beautiful woman. He was attracted to her and could not forget her face. He craved her presence all the time. He was so obsessive about her that he began ignoring everything and started looking for her. Finally, he found her in a remote forest. He approached her, explained his love for her, and begged her to love him. Finally, the young woman agreed to love him. Months passed. The young man had forgotten his duties and even his mother. His mother kept looking for him. Finally, the young woman got bored of him and wanted to get rid of him. She told him to go home, hoping that he would not show up again. With difficulty, he agreed to go home but said he would come back soon. He went back home but could not stay away. He went back again to his lady.

This happened so many times that the young woman became frustrated and actually wanted to get rid of him. Finally, she said, "For us to live together forever and to stay young forever, we need your mother's heart. Come back only if can get your mother's heart." This man's love was so blind that he agreed to come back with his mother's heart.

He started going home, thinking only about the young lady. He finally reached the house, and without hesitation, he told his mother what happened, saying that he cannot exist without that woman. His mother tried to explain that as time passed, things would settle down; she also offered to talk to the young woman and see whether she could convince her. But he was restless and did not listen to his mother's words.

Finally, he killed his mother without thinking, rationalizing the truth within the young woman's words. He killed his mother, took her heart, and ran back toward the forest with the heart in a bag. He suddenly tripped over a rock and fell to the ground, crying out loudly and spontaneously saying, "Mom!" with a pain in his leg. From within the bag, the mother's heart said, "Be careful, son, you have to live a long and healthy life; accept my blessings too."

While this is an extreme example of passion, love, emotions, and uncontrolled instincts, it shows that there are both negative and positive forces within us. The man was not evil. He was morally good, innocent and living happily with his mother. He could have had expected marriage, children, and a fresh life. But his extreme passion, an irresistible instinct, became a negative force that drove him out of his place and made him obsessive and immoral.

We lose judgment and wisdom when we are emotional. Passions and desires cloud our conscious decision making.

A mother's love for her son is extreme; if not in this story, it is proved on many other occasions. There is no alternative to a mother's love; even after she was killed for another young woman's love, her heart longed for her son's happiness; she could not tolerate her son being hurt. That may be too extreme, but we do see this extreme love in history on several occasions.

Finally, the young lady thought only about herself and how to get rid of him, rather than thinking about his obsessive, irrational thinking. He was even willing to go back to bring his mother's heart. She did not think about the consequences that can happen. People consider many different ways to resolve the issues, but she was too extreme in her way to get rid of him.

This story is just an example of extreme feelings and impulses; we are now going to discuss the common forces within that are both positive and negative and how to balance them with harmony between our conscious and subconscious minds.

Common Negative (Opposing) Forces

- Easy frustration, impulsiveness

- Hopelessness, depression, anxiety, restlessness, irritability

- Not able to concentrate, helplessness, obsessiveness, compulsiveness

- Easy anger, fear, shyness, guilt, grudge building

- Not able to control substance abuse, peer pressure

- Irrational thinking

- Ignorance

- Criticizing others

- Harshness in speaking

- Misconduct

- Resentment

- Prejudice

- Betrayal

- Unrealistic expectations

- Hurting others

- Being sad and down in the dumps

- Easily crying

- Some other feelings are

- "I am bad."

- "I am a burden."

- "I am a failure."

- "I lost my will to live."

- "I cannot sleep."

"Revenge" and "enemy" are not my favorite words. The best revenge one can get on one's enemy is by living a happy, healthy, and prosperous life. But that may make your opponent envy you and build a grudge against you, which are not desirable either. So not to keep suffer from those nasty opposing forces, the best advice is, do not allow the arrows of negative forces to flow freely in either way. Simply let them go. Forgiveness is the best option.

COMMON POSITIVE (PRODUCTIVE) FORCES

- Aspire to change

- Accept what you are now

- Want to get better

- Crave to get better by all means

- Get self-control

- Respect others and their feelings

- Make family and other people happy

- Be responsible for one's own actions

- Stay clean and productive

- Be an example to others as good and helpful

- Be calm, quiet, and peaceful

- Do not mix logic with emotions

- Show love and compassion

- Have a subdued nature

- Forgive

- Adapt

- Solve problems

- Be creative

- Acknowledge shortcomings and mistakes

- Think positive

- Smile and laugh

- Accept change

- Be motivated

- Have patience

- Prevent problems

- Understand others and see commonality

- Trust

I strongly believe that most of these negative and positive forces are due to familial and genetic nature of our personalities, with circumstances added to them. But once we realize this, we have plenty of opportunity to make ourselves better. We can eliminate some negative forces and nurture some positive ones, and overall, we can optimize all the forces.

In the desert, there was a lone bird trying to fly to a nearby town. It became thirsty, and there was no water around. While gazing down, it saw a pot on the ground with a narrow neck. It eagerly flew over and looked inside. There was some water, but all the way down, it could not reach it with its beak. It needed to act quickly. It could not hold onto its thirst and could not fly fast enough to reach a nearby water hole without quenching its thirst first.

It started picking up small stones and dropped them into the jar's narrow neck one by one, until the water rose to the top as the stones filled the jar. It happily quenched its thirst and continued on its way.

This story reminds us of the pearl; we have positive forces within us all the time, but they may be dominated by negative thoughts on the surface. We need to remove the negative forces one by one until we reach the positive aspects.

Positive and negative forces are within us at conscious and subconscious levels. But if they are in disharmony, whatever is the dominating impulse will show up in our actions as the main force, driving them toward their corresponding actions. If you have more negative forces occupying your thoughts, your actions will prove that and lead to certain consequences.

As long as you realize this and practice to keep them in harmony, you can succeed.

Some qualities do not fall into either positive or negative forces. They also do not belong to one personality type. We see them in very successful, influential people too. These qualities do not have any preference to gender, age, place, or where they came from. They include but not limited to envy, jealousy, and ego. People with these qualities often praise themselves or want others to do so. Also, they are suspicious and cannot tolerate others being happy. They are self-centered in nature and feel that others are always wrong in their opinion.

They do not feel any sympathy for others. They feel that they know everything, and they always seek attention. They are also closed-minded with too much self-pride. While some personality disorders fall within these qualities, we often do not recognize the people who have these qualities, even if we are close to them. Some people attribute them as good qualities due to their successful life. Other qualities include when it comes to actually helping others, they do not. Their words and actions do not meet.

They may not accept the need to transform themselves, but if they realize their qualities, they can shed them one by one with practice. I believe they are mostly a mixed bag of personalities, and they are more common among some communities and cultures than others. This could be one of those "survival of the fittest" features.

Positive Reinforcement

Practice with consistency, as the saying goes: Start doing meditation with honesty, self-improvement, and dedication.

> **Chaos is inherent in all compounded things.
> Strive on with diligence.—Buddha**

Brain and Plasticity (Self-Healing)

Plasticity is the ability to change or rewire the brain; the ability to adapt to disease.

Healthy people have the same number of brain cells at birth as in adulthood, but those cells grow in size, reaching maximum size at about age six. Neuroplasticity is the brain's ability to reorganize, adapt, and compensate for environmental changes or disease.

"Plasticity" is defined as any enduring change in cortical properties as per strength of internal connections, neuronal properties, and pattern of representations and controls. Basically, brain functions are reorganized as much as possible to accommodate new needs or regain the function of lost cells.

New discoveries and research show that the brain has a greater ability to redevelop, reorganize, and help damaged areas than previously believed.

The mind and the brain use their coping skills, which involve physical action, mental efforts, and supplementary acts, to help neuromodulation and neuroplasticity.

New connections are created every time we remember something or have a new thought. Stronger, more intense emotional connections are linked to memories, prompted by repeatedly stimulating thoughts.

Sleep is probably the best time for the brain to consolidate memory, and new learned things stay there.

When we think positively, the brain can overcome 50 to 70 percent of symptoms. Eat right and eat well; that will have positive effects on the brain.

A Brief Note on Enlightenment

Enlightenment is rare phenomena. Buddha did not know that his long meditation would take him (after six years) to enlightenment. He retained the benefits of meditation forever, but he still practiced daily, just to enjoy the feeling of meditation and its benefits.

Like a bird flies without leaving tracks in the sky, no one else can take another person to the state of mind of nothingness or emptiness.

People can tell you how to initiate the practice of meditation and how to be persistent in its practice, but the path to enlightenment is anybody's guess.

But long before enlightenment itself, Buddha knew his goals, his questions, and his quest for answers. He also determined not to give up. Meditation was there long before Buddha, but he became synonymous with meditation with his enlightenment and persistence. His teachings mainly involved meditation as the way to self-help and happiness. After those six years and after finding answers to his burning questions, he was able to formulate many new philosophical thoughts and practices. So only after he reached his targeted goals, he was able to bring so much of new thought and practice. He was able to bring the benefit of his enlightenment to the whole world.

In a similar way, our goal at this point is not empty minded meditation, but goal-oriented practice, training our brain to rewire and remodulate and get the benefit of neural plasticity so we can get better faster.

If we practice meditation consistently and go into Buddha-type of meditation, we will get enormous benefits. But we lose nothing if we cannot reach that higher state of mind. If we can calm down the mind and keep it in its place with mindfulness by consistent practice, it will do good for our body, brain, and mind, and it will make us recover faster. Even trying to reach the state of emptiness will reward us with many benefits in all aspects of life.

Self-Realization

In fact, these were the last words of Buddha: "practice with diligence" (careful and persistent work/effort or persevere in carrying out tasks/duties). After that, he slipped into a coma and died. He likely had either GI bleeding due to a peptic ulcer or gastroenteritis and dysentery due to food poisoning.

But Buddha did not have any problems to begin with. When he was twenty-nine, he had a newborn infant son, a wife, and a small kingdom. He was physically healthy, but he could not have a peaceful mind; he had obsessive thoughts, with restless and burning questions regarding life and the sufferings that humans go through. He also wanted to find the answers on how to minimize suffering. He was the first behavioral therapist. Over the six years of his search for truth, he had plenty of frustration, disappointments, and discouragement, along with physical pain and hunger. But he never gave up. Once he looked inside his own mind, he found the answers, and he never suffered again. Nothing was able to bother him anymore.

EQUANIMITY (HOMEOSTASIS)

This is a balanced mind/soul in any extreme or conventional circumstances. It is a state of psychological stability and composure, which is undisturbed by exposure to emotions, pain, or other phenomena that may cause others to lose the balance of their mind. The virtue and value of equanimity is great. It is said that true equanimity is a greater virtue than enlightenment. It is as difficult as keeping a boat standing still in the middle of a stormy ocean. Achieving equanimity with practice will do immense help in all aspects of life.

MODERATION/BALANCE

Moderation is considered a key part of one's personal development. There is nothing that cannot be moderated, including one's actions, desires, and even thoughts.

It is believed that by being in balance, one achieves a more natural state, faces less resistance in life, and recognizes one's true limits. Taken to the extreme, moderation is complex and can be difficult, not only to accept but also to understand and implement.

Meditation Uses

In the current day and age of a disharmonious environment and life styles of overindulgence, preserving and protecting health through meditation is extremely useful. Meditation also helps us to recover from pain and disease, to have a calm and tranquilizing life, and to release us from anxiety, worries, and addictions.

Recent research shows that embryos start crying at the age of twenty-eight weeks, inside the uterus. A study done to assess the effects on babies of cocaine and tobacco use found that the fetus responds to sudden sounds by crying: the chin trembles, the body jerks, and the mouth opens. Initially, this was thought to be seizures but later was confirmed as crying. As an adult, let us try to be joyful during the rest of our life through meditation.

Practice

Frequently, patients in group therapy express their inner feelings and their motivations regarding how they are going to clean up once they leave treatment and start a fresh new life, hoping never to return to the hospital as patients.

We are often quite surprised with their inner brilliance, how they communicate their ideas, how well they present themselves consciously. Sometimes they present themselves with simple art and drawings.

Sometimes during sessions, they even start advising other patients, telling them about their coping skills and explaining how to get better in tough situations. They show consistency at each stage in the therapy sessions.

Once they are discharged, we do not know what happens. Why do things go wrong? Many of them return with the same symptoms, often getting worse after discharge. They stop taking their medicine and cannot keep from indulging in activities they are not supposed to do. They succumb to peer pressure, cannot endure family and personal struggles, cannot find a job, and cannot keep up their skills. They often come back feeling the best comfort in the hospital again.

We can understand their inability to continue their medication. Even well-controlled depression can recur once medication is stopped in more than 50 percent of patients. But in just a few months after discharge, many patients come back to the hospital. We notice there are other reasons besides just stopping the medication.

The most common reason is that they believe they lack the practice to sustain their gains. We try to arrange continuation of group therapies; we advise them about Alcoholics Anonymous, Narcotics Anonymous, and other groups where they can get sustained support, but most of them fail to attend them or do not make an effort to go. The main reason identified is lack of sustained motivation because of lack of practice. Practice makes perfect, and they ignore that. They come to the conclusion that their illness is over; they feel on top of the world when the hospital door opens out.

Today I saw a twenty-seven-year-old male. He was expelled from a drug rehab program because of aggressive behavior toward others and a sudden explosive tendency.

After going home, he felt more frustration and overdosed on his prescription medications. He called his mother about it, but there were no serious consequences, and now he was back in the psychiatric hospital. As he spoke, he sounded like a gentle man. He already had a bachelor's degree in psychology and economics and planned to get a master's in psychology. Meanwhile, he could not control his behavioral tendencies; he used drugs like heroin and opiates. He had been in psychiatric hospitals in the past and was now here after the drug rehabilitation program.

He had failed , but I was sure he was not going to give up. After talking to him, I felt some of his behavioral traits may not be in his control, and he needed a lot of medication and ancillary services on a consistent basis. But with consistency in his treatment plans, he could succeed to a greater extent.

Once there was a king known for his laziness. He was curious to know whether anybody else in his kingdom was lazier than him.

He summoned his officers and ordered them to call for a competition. After a few months, the news reached throughout his kingdom, and many aspirants arrived in the capital. The day of competitions came. Everybody assembled in the main hall. The official conducting the program announced independent tests, with questions to prove each competitor's laziness. Finally, it was time to choose the winner. The king came onto the stage and asked everyone to raise their hand if they thought they were the laziest of all. Every competitor but one did so.

The king became curious and asked the man who had not raised his hand, "Why did you come all this way, spending months to travel to the city from a remote place, but did not raise your hand to compete?"

The man said, "I feel too lazy to raise my hand or say that I am lazy."

The king was remarkably intelligent and knew the genuineness in this person's claim. The really lazy person does not care about the consequences and does not care about losses. He will drop anything and everything for his laziness.

So the king made him the winner.

Here, laziness is a pathetic quality. But the man had traveled and participated in the competition with effort, and he became the winner, fulfilling his targeted goal.

Remember, our goals are important, despite the obstacles. Do not give up.

This "Reveal" is a small but sincere effort to stress the importance of practice, practice, practice (consistency is the key to success) to show our potential, to continue to achieve forever, and to give us a very balanced life.

I have not failed 10,000 times. I have successfully found 10,000 ways that will not work.—Thomas Edison

SELF-EXPLORING NATURE

Patience comes to those who wait. Find the key to yourself, and every door in the world will open.

Chance favors the prepared mind.—Louis Pasteur

A pharmaceutical company selected ten drug addicts to take part in a study. After their recovery program, based on their skills, they were trained and placed in jobs. Out of the ten, eight of them quit their jobs by the end of the first year and went back to taking drugs. The ninth one did the same in the second year. The tenth person is still working for the same company, with the same enthusiasm, and he does not mind sharing his story with everyone. He is actually working for a company that makes drugs that counteract addiction.

We are not looking for perfection, at least at this point. Consistent practice, not giving up, and a goal-oriented approach are our priority.

For example, you may have a great idea or invention or improvement for an existing product. It is good to have the idea but not enough. You have to plan how to implement that idea into reality. You must turn that idea into a product and promote it into the market. You have to contact the necessary people to turn the idea into a product. Until then, having the idea is great, but it does not result in an actual product.

But the product of self-realization and the improvement that comes from meditation and self-exploration will create a whole lot. By improving your thoughts, it will provide a new perspective and energy to the brain, with additional outcomes.

One way to say it is that by itself, the concept is the result.

When meditating, do not force your mind. If it wants to wander, let it be, but do not give up meditation. One day the mind will lose the wandering part and feel empty, and that is meditation.

"Success is not how far you get, but the distance you traveled from where you started." -- Unknown source.

A long time ago, there was a physician who was new to town. He started his practice in an office building. The doctor interviewed and hired one young lady as his secretary.

The young woman did her job very elegantly; she spoke eloquently, was quiet, had adequate skills, and was impressive overall.

Eventually, she revealed to the doctor that she had dropped out of high school. During that time, she had a lot of issues.

Now she is working here in doctor's office but that was not her passion; She wanted to work as a bartender or waitress.She was irresistibly attracted to people with unusual habits and odd looks. She was drawn to people who used alcohol and other recreational drugs. This sounded strange to the doctor, because he did not find her that delinquent in the office. She was a lot better than other workers.

After working there a year, she told the doctor that she was moving away with her new boyfriend. The doctor wished her good luck and promised to take her back if she ever came back to town.

Years passed; the doctor often thought about her and hoped she was doing great wherever she was. He used to remember the Sigmund Freud quote: "What does a woman want?" But this girl had told him directly what she wanted and what her choices were. He wondered if that was her real choice or if she was unable to see the real truth of what she wanted?

When the doctor was in his seventies, he semiretired. One day as he was leaving his office, he saw a fragile-looking, debilitated woman in the waiting hall. He immediately recognized her. He sat down with her, and they began talking about what had happened over all the years with her and her children and her father.

She said that her father likely died naturally, and she had not had any contact with her children and was not able to trace where they were. With communications not well established at that time, it was difficult.

She explained that after a few years, she started going on long road trips with the bike gang, leaving the children behind with her father or her first ex-husband.

A few more years passed with more and more troubles. All her bad habits came back, including drugs and alcohol. She slowly became the property of the gangs. Once, she used to listen to her own instincts and had her own opinions, but no more. She had no opinion on anything. She was abused in many ways, by many people. She wanted to escape and come back but was not able to do so. Finally, one day in a campground, she became very ill, and nobody cared for her.

A strange-looking guy had joined the gang. She had observed that he often looked at her with interest. Everybody made comments about him, ridiculing him, because he looked odd to the other gang members. But he stayed with them.

When she became sick, the gang left the campground without taking her with them. She became delirious and found herself in a hospital, without knowing how she got there. It took fifteen days to recover.

She asked the nurse how she came to the hospital. The nurse explained that a strange-looking man had brought her to the emergency room. He stayed in the room with her, took care of her, and then just left after she recovered. He did not leave any details on how to find him.

When she was discharged, she did not know what to do; she looked around for the man who had brought her to the hospital, but there was no trace of him.

She walked around the streets near the hospital. She found a group home for the mentally challenged and physically disabled; some of the people who lived there had cerebral palsy, others were born with serious birth defects, and others were mentally disabled and needed total care. She went inside and asked for work. There was an opening, so they asked her to stay and help take care of the residents. Eventually, she was able to help those who needed total care. Each time she looked at them, she felt like she was looking at herself. She had been born normal and grew up with a loving father. Her father paid attention to her, gave her love and kindness, and sent her to school. He went to all her activities as much as possible, but still she had made all the wrong choices, made bad decisions, and went in the wrong directions.

She had abused her character, both physically and mentally, and she had insulted her own attitude, dignity, and self-esteem. There was nothing left to say. She wondered who was worse off, a person born with physical or mental disabilities, which is not their fault, or a person who destroyed herself, despite having so much available to her.

Some of the residents of the group home may not have been born with problems if their mothers had taken care of themselves while they were pregnant. They may have abused alcohol (resulting in fetal alcohol syndrome), smoked, or did drugs. While mistreating their bodies, they did not even care for the baby inside their womb, she thought.

She liked working in the group home, and as the months passed, she had no desire to go back to her old life.

She did not cry; she felt like there was nothing else for her to do. *Who should I cry for?* she thought. *I did not care for my children when they needed me. I did not help my father in his last days. Crying at this point only shows another weakness.* With that she thought, *I should go back to my hometown and attempt to see them once more. I should take all this with a nonemotional nature and not create any ripples in my children's lives.* With that, she had caught the doctor up on her past.

"The first person I recalled was you, Doctor," she continued. "I remember you tried to inculcate good values in me every time we conversed. You respected me. I thought at least I should see you once for my satisfaction, so I'm here today. Thanks for listening; it means a lot to me," she concluded.

The doctor thanked her for remembering him this long, thanked her for her self-realization, and asked her where she was now staying.

She said that she was staying in a small motel near the office building.

After their conversation was over, the doctor asked her to come to his house. She refused, saying that she would stay in the motel. The doctor offered to drop her at the motel and pick her up tomorrow, when they could start making inquiries about her children's whereabouts. They would try to locate them and see if she could meet with them.

She thanked him for the idea and said she would try to find them on her own, adding that she would see him again in the office soon.

The doctor left the office and drove home, thinking about her. He believed that the quote "The predetermined soul will reach its predetermined destiny" may be true.

The next morning, he worked briefly in his office and then started driving back home. There was a lot of commotion in the area, and he saw police vehicles and an ambulance.

The doctor stopped his car and got out. Everyone was heading toward the motel, so he went there also. He wondered if anything had happened to his former assistant. In the motel, police had found someone who had died peacefully in her bed, with no suggestion of suicide, no poison or drugs in the room, and no other information to trace her relatives or friends. After searching her belongings, police found her name, and the doctor identified her as well. He told the police that he had known her for the last thirty years, adding that she had just come to meet him yesterday He told the police briefly about her situation. Before the police took her away, the doctor told them he would take care of her funeral expenses.

While waiting for the postmortem report, the doctor wondered what had happened to her. She had been sick and recovered from a serious infection; perhaps an infection had lingered in her body, causing her death. Could a pulmonary embolism or heart attack have occurred? A brain bleed or stroke may have happened, or she could have suddenly gone into sepsis. Did she commit suicide? It did not matter at this point.

While awaiting the postmortem report, which would provide some facts regarding the reasons for her death, the doctor wondered,

"Was she content as she breathed her last breath?" Her death had happened suddenly, and the only thing that mattered was if she had been content. The summary of her whole life experience was in that last breath; contentment, satisfaction, and achievement are all that matter as we consciously leave this world.

No one wants to die. We want to live forever if possible. But when it is time to leave behind everything, we hope to take that last breath with contentment. Many people who lose consciousness in their last minutes do not know that they are dying. Buddha slipped into a coma and was not aware of his last breath. But he blessed people until his last moment of consciousness. People in their last moments hope to pay attention to their whole life summary. While seeing loved ones for a last time, we leave them with memories, achievements, and love. But taking that last breath with contentment while leaving this world is a valuable asset to the remaining family members.

The doctor learned from the postmortem report that there were no traces of poisons or drugs in her system; there were no signs of strangulation, heart attack, blood clots in the lungs, or stroke. No signs suggested infection or tissue damage. Overall, it was a natural cause of death, not a suicide, infection, or disease.

The report said the cause of death was unknown. The doctor was quite satisfied that she had left this world with contentment, and her soul had reached its destiny in peace. He got the utmost satisfaction of caring for her in her last day on this earth.

He told himself that she was not alone; he had been there for her. She probably left her last breath with the same feeling that she was not alone.

It is not surprising that many people we see as misguided and lost were forced by negative impulses to act.

People seldom improve when they have no other model but themselves to copy after.—Oliver Goldsmith

This quote may be true, but sometimes, even if we have many role models and good people around, we cannot see them due to strong opposing forces governing our minds, which blindfold us.

This woman was not able to consistently maintain the positive forces in her life; due to lack of practice, she couldn't overcome her impulses. Also, her internal conflict created disharmony between positive and negative impulses, and her negative forces always dominated.

LOST MY BUDDHA

A while ago, my best friend died. He was my wholesome counselor and was always there whenever I needed him. I could talk to him without any hesitation. Every time I felt that I had lost my spirit and direction. After he died, the first thing I felt, other than sympathy for his family, was, "I lost my Buddha." The question remained: who was there to help me out? One day, I looked inside myself and realized that I had my Buddha in me. After that, I regained my positive thoughts and confidence. So, like Buddha said, we all can become Buddha at different levels of enlightenment, as long as we look inside of our mind and practice with diligence. Our Buddha goes with us, with our body, and we have it until our last breath.

As time passes, new technologies will evolve; some may be able to eradicate diseases or make the mind happier by erasing all our worries. But until then, looking within ourselves, practicing with diligence, and meditation are the best solution to everyone and at all times.

PLAN OF ACTION

Practice is our mode of action. Observe mindfully all the negative and positive forces inside that you are struggling with.

Understand each other's needs, and learn which ones should be eliminated. Write down all your negative forces that are dominating you and bothering you and hindering your progress. Let go of past events, with no rumination. Start communicating consciously with your subconscious mind. If your mind wanders at the beginning, let it be.

Evaluate yourself time and again, like doing a project. Work consistently until consistency prevails in your thoughts. Work toward positive goals only. Habituate your mind with positive thoughts only; that is our meditation for now. We are not looking for enlightenment or empty mindedness.

Your mind will slowly start to settle down and wander less and less, as long as you don't give up your positive thoughts and practice. Make adequate time for relaxation and develop good sleep habits. Stay away from all unhealthy substances. Do not blame anyone, including yourself, for anything. Stop the blame game.

Say "Let it go" each time you start to blame the past or anybody else. Follow your medical treatment, if any. Look from a broader perspective to see if you need help. In some cases, medication is a part of life, something you need on a daily basis, just like food.

Maintain a list of the real issues. From time to time, reevaluate the negative forces driving your actions. Discover the benefits of consistent practice. Don't give up; let your conscious efforts combine with your subconscious mind.

Slowly, you will see positive forces appear one by one in your thoughts and actions in the form of less anger, no grudges, less envy, and subdued emotions; you will also see more love, patience, compassion, rationality, motivation, and drive. You will begin to pursue goals and happiness for your loved ones and ultimately yourself.

Mind

REMEMBER, WE CREATE OUR selves constantly as we go along.

Defined by many in different ways, we can call it the cognitive part of the human brain.

It is formless, indeterminate, not made of any material or perceivable with any senses.

What is the spirit and expression of the brain or understanding, knowledge, or awareness? I do not know, but the best description of the mind I ever heard was from a Telugu Lyricist Acharya Atreya in his song(*Mouname Nee Basha O Mooga Manasa*)with English translation as below:

"The one with its own silent language
Is the grand canyon of imagination
The cradle of temptations
The demon of mischievous
For one mistake, it can repent life long
The greatest stage for drama
An untied free flying kite

Doesn't acknowledge, forgets the things that it got
Always craves for the things it does not have
The creature of desires
The angel of creativity"

There is a delicate balance between the brain and its invisible, mysterious, yet acknowledgeable partner, the mind. They both embody the soul that our body hosts from birth to death.

They try to live in harmony with natural resources, and as we grow with day-by-day influences, they try to develop and satisfy the needs of each other. So many external influences ,foods, drinks, stress, environment, climate, physical illness, trauma, and infections try to take away that delicate balance.

We try to maintain that balance to keep the human body and ultimately the soul happy with peace and health.

Can we help our brain and mind together in these modern times, to help them develop and stay strong, to maintain their harmony, to function at the best possible optimal level?

To do that, many of us need some life style changes including diet, sleep, and exercise. We also need to rigorously train our mind and develop some voluntary control. Setting limits and remembering its own limitations is necessary, so that it will not strain the brain and ultimately ruin the relationship and make our soul suffer. For that, we need to know first of all what we are and what we do on a daily basis. We also need to know how to eat, rest, and take care of our precious body that harbors the brain, the mind, and ultimately the soul.

Take a moment to explore your self. It takes only a few days to research what is going on with our life style, needs, dislikes, likes, and what we are overdoing or neglecting.

Unfortunately, sometimes we are affected by diseases from external, genetic, or environmental influences that are not in our control. How do we come out of them and bounce back? Good health also requires practice and patience.

The definition of health is "a sound mind in a sound body." How can we achieve this and maintain it? If factors that are not in our control are overwhelming our body, brain, and mind, how can we reach our optimal goals to stay comfortable, functional, and yet joyful and purposeful?

For that, we need to know what our body is composed of, and what it needs on a consistent basis.

The overall representation of our soul is the expression of the combined efforts of the brain and mind, and it depends on how carefully we take care of ourselves. Throughout our life, it depends on practice of mind, brain, and body. Abusing our physical body and mind is like destroying our brain (or at least not maintaining it properly). So no more good can come out of it. A healthy mind in a healthy body is well suited here.

MIND AND BRAIN DIET

Think positive. Train your brain with positive ways. If you do so, the brain can overcome most symptoms. Eat well and eat right, and it will have positive effects on your brain and body and ultimately lead to pleasure. Rest well and adequately, both physically and mentally. Know that a sensitive balance exists between optimal, balanced functioning of mood, mind, and the environment.

A wise person once said, "Hunger does not know the taste. Sleep does not know the luxury."

This is particularly true. If we eat only when we are hungry, and sleep only when we are tired, everything will be well done. With current societal events and time demands, we have to plan when to eat and sleep. We eat with plenty of choices around us without control.

Moderation/Balance: Moderation is considered a vital part of one's personal development. There is nothing that cannot be moderated, including one's actions, one's desires, and even one's thoughts.

There is no strict diet program that is written in stone. No single program is best for everyone. People are rarely able to continue to certain diets or food specifics. There is so much of variety of food. All of us desire to experience the range and consider the choices that we have.

With moderation, we can enjoy the things that we like without any hesitation or regret. Moderation is the way in dietary practice, just like any other practice. Remember, not too tight, not too loose. The same principle applies: "not too little, not too much." Adequate but moderate choice is the solution for any diet program. Knowing what you need to eat is most useful when practicing moderation. You can be picky about the items that your body and brain need as basic food elements and daily requirements.

The tongue, with its two main functions of speech and taste, is extremely difficult for the mind to control. Many of us fail to control our speech and control our food intake; it requires thriving practice.

Part Two

Brain Diet

The only way to keep your health is to eat what you do not want, drink what you do not like, and do what you would rather not.—Mark Twain

UNTIL WE INNOVATE, WE may at least improve.

The body was never meant to be treated as a refuse bin, holding all the foods that the palate demands.—Mahatma Gandhi

Our body is made up of water and different materials that form proteins, carbohydrates, and fats, along with minerals and vitamins, all from the ground in one form or another. We function as a human body and brain, with the support of synchronous activity of neurotransmitters and hormones that are made from different elements.

In order to properly maintain our body and brain, and to keep them functioning properly, we need approximately two thousand calories daily. These calories come from various forms of foods and are part of the daily maintenance requirements. Ideally, foods contain almost everything that we need on a daily basis. People often eat in excess, and we often eat foods that are not healthy. Trying them is different from habitually overeating or consistently choosing the wrong foods.

Certain health conditions, especially those connected to the brain or the mind, require particular attention. Consuming the right daily intake of food and nutrients is essential, as is avoiding foods that are harmful. To keep the body healthy, along with a healthy brain and mood, use precaution when deciding what to eat. There are also endogenous, genetic, familial, and exogenous causes that predispose us for disease. With good dietary habits, and persistence of practice through meditation, we can limit a disease's harmful effects and survive in a healthy state with a healthy mind. Through meditation and by using the capabilities of neural plasticity of the brain and nervous system, we can achieve this.

This section discusses dietary issues pertaining to brain and meditation. For other dietary guidelines, many other resources are available.

What the Brain Needs

A healthy body: The body is the sanctum sanctorum of your soul and mind. Care for it well. Respect your brain and soul by respecting your body. Do not indulge in anything to excess. Excessive laziness, too much wear and tear, too much sleep, too little sleep, inadequate eating, excess eating, excessive drinking, using depressants or stimulants, and taking unnecessary medicines all disrespect your soul, brain, and mind. Keep everything in moderation and show keen attention to daily activities. Live with flexibility.

Your brain has certain nutritional needs. The brain represents only 2 percent of the body weight, but it receives 15 percent of the cardiac output, consumes 20 percent of the body's oxygen, and uses 25 percent of the body's glucose. With a global blood flow of 57 ml/100 grams per minute, the brain extracts approximately 50 percent of oxygen and 10 percent of glucose from the arterial blood.

Glucose can be incorporated into lipids, proteins, and glycogen, and it is also the precursor of gamma aminobutyric acid (GABA), glutamate, and of neurotransmitters such as acetylcholine.

The brain organizes various functions of the body. Most are of a cognitive nature or concern the regulation of the motor system.

The energy consumption of the brain is exceptionally high. It consumes 20 percent of the carbohydrates ingested over a twenty-four-hour period. This corresponds to 100 grams of glucose per day or half of the daily requirement for a human being. An average young person's brain consumes approximately 200 grams of glucose per day.

The brain is exclusively dependent on glucose as an energy source. Lactate and betahydroxybutyric acid can also be considered as substrates but only under certain conditions of considerable stress levels or malnutrition. Also, the brain is separated from the rest of the body's circulation by the blood-brain barrier. Blood glucose has to be brought there via a specific transporter system.

The brain maintains its own glucose content and needs. The brain is always supplied with more energy than the body in extreme stress situations. In overweight individuals, the brain's energy distribution mechanism is disrupted. With chronic stress, the energy flux between the brain and the body is diverted, a phenomenon that can lead to obesity.

The brain gets a portion of its energy from ketones.(ketone bodies are three compounds that are produced as by-products when fatty acids are broken down for energy in the liver. Two of the three are used as a source of energy in the heart and brain while the third (acetone) is a waste product excreted from the body. In the brain, they are a vital source of energy during fasting Although termed "bodies", they are dissolved substances, not particles(from wikipedia). When glucose is not available during fasting or strenuous exercise, the body's carbohydrate level drops. In the event of low blood glucose, other tissues have additional energy sources besides ketones, such as fatty acids, but the brain does not. After the diet has been changed, and the blood glucose stays lower for three days, the brain gets 25 percent of its energy from ketone bodies. After about four days, this goes up to 70 percent. During the initial stages, the brain does not burn ketones since they are an important substrate for lipid synthesis in the brain.

DIETS OF SOME GREAT PEOPLE (WIKIPEDIA)

Thomas Edison lived last few years of his life consuming milk for liquids. He thought would live longer just with milk. This proved to be wrong, and there was no scientific backing either. Edison was said to have been influenced by a popular fad diet. In his last few years, "the only liquid he consumed was a pint of milk every three hours." He is reported to have believed this diet would restore his health. However, this tale is doubtful. In 1930, the year before Edison died, Mina, his wife said in an interview about him, "Correct eating is one of his greatest hobbies." Edison's last breath is reportedly contained in a test tube at the Henry Ford Museum.

Ford reportedly convinced Charles Edison, son of Thomas Edison (the 42nd governor of New Jersey) to seal a test tube of air in the inventor's room shortly after his death, as a memento.

Steve Jobs (February 24, 1955–October 5, 2011) was an American entrepreneur and inventor, best known as the cofounder, chairman, and CEO of Apple Inc. Through Apple, he was widely recognized as a charismatic pioneer of the personal computer revolution and for his influential career in the computer and consumer electronics fields. Jobs also cofounded and served as chief executive of Pixar Animation Studios. He became a member of the board of directors of the Walt Disney Company in 2006, when Disney acquired Pixar.

Despite following strict dietary protocols, Jobs developed cancer, and surgical approaches failed to keep him alive. He had a tendency to eat only one or two types of food, like carrots or apples, for weeks at a time. There are other health issues that can arise from adhering to such a limited diet.

Yoshiro Nakamatsu (Born June 26, 1928): Also known as Dr. Naka Mats, this Japanese inventor of floppy discs, CDs, and many other items consumes only seven hundred calories per day. He follows a strict diet protocol with no coffee, tea, or alcohol. He eats only once a day. He uses many brain stimulating devices to sharpen his thoughts.

Buddha followed no dietary restrictions other than moderation of the total food intake. He ate anything and everything given to him. His last meal contained pork. He ate only once a day, around 11:00 a.m. Most likely, the foods he ate were limited in calories. He enjoyed food and ate as much as he could in his one meal per day. This was especially true when he was a guest in a village or the king's palace. He ate well. He practiced two hours of meditation each day, along with a simple walk. This was in addition to walking from town to town to teach and deliver sermons.

Buddha followed the principle of moderation with flexibility in every aspect of his life: "Do not pull the string too tight, it will break; do not keep the string too loose, it will not give the tune." That is the concept he followed in his every action.

Albert Einstein was a vegetarian only for the last year or so of his life, though he appears to have supported the idea for many years before practicing it himself. He said, "So I am living without fats, without meat, without fish, but am feeling quite well this way. It always seems that man was not born to be a carnivore." Einstein was a heavy smoker but did not drink alcohol.

> **I have always eaten animal flesh with a somewhat guilty conscience.—Albert Einstein**

> **It is my view that the vegetarian manner of living by its purely physical effect on the human temperament would most beneficially influence the lot of mankind.—Albert Einstein (in a letter to Vegetarian WatchTower, December 27, 1930)**

> **It is health that is real wealth, not peaces of gold and silver.—Mahatma Gandhi**

> **I hold flesh-food to be unsuited to our species.—Mahatma Gandhi**

Mahatma Gandhi believed that food was an integral part of shaping our consciousness and not just meant to satiate our hunger. He experimented throughout his life to find his "perfect diet," an experiment that lasted over thirty-five years. Earlier in his life, he consumed meat only on a few occasions. He stopped eating meat and was a complete vegetarian by 1906.

Bill Gates (Born October 28, 1955) is an American business magnate and philanthropist. Gates is the former chief executive and current chairman of Microsoft, the world's largest computer software company. He is consistently ranked among the world's wealthiest people. He has also written several books. Gates has pursued a number of philanthropic endeavors, donating large amounts of money to various charitable organizations and scientific research programs through the Bill & Melinda Gates Foundation, established in 2000.

Gates recently said, "The future of meat is vegan. I do not regard flesh food as necessary for us at any stage and under any clime in which it is possible for human beings ordinarily to live."

Joanne K. Rowling (Born July 31, 1965), pen name J. K. Rowling, is a British novelist, best known as the author of the *Harry Potter* fantasy series. The *Potter* books have gained worldwide attention, won multiple awards, and sold more than 400 million copies. They have become the best-selling book series in history and are the basis for the highest-grossing film series in history.

To my knowledge, no particular dietary pattern influenced her creativity or imagination. It is self-motivation and spontaneity. We should consider analyzing her brain images for Einstein-like convolutions or any other distinctive patterns.

Tips to Control Eating

The goal is to reduce our desire for food (we eat more than we need in most cases).

- Eat slowly and small amounts each time. Try to use a small fork or spoon if possible.

- Do not take a second serving of the same food item.

- Try to limit cooking to just a few items per day (less variety is good if you want to eat less).

- Eat consciously; do not do anything else while eating.

- Just like using the bedroom only for sleeping as part of sleep hygiene, make a habit of eating in one single area, such as the dining table.

- Spend less time in the kitchen.

- Keep fewer snacks available in the house.

- Put food away, in its place, and not in sight.

- Keep a food plate or food pyramid poster in the dining room or kitchen.

Chewing

Some research suggests chewing each bite of food for thirty seconds. While we need not count each time, chewing longer helps digestion by mixing the food with saliva in the mouth before it reaches the stomach, where it has already been grinded well. It will be absorbed faster and more.

Research has found that chewing longer can help people eat less, and they become thinner.

PRECAUTIONS

Make sure that your diet is low in calories. If your diet is loaded with calories and you spend more time at the dining table, you will likely consume more than necessary. The additional consumption means more and more calories. Normally, chewing longer does not make healthy people tire easily, and they certainly can complete their meal. People with myasthenia gravis or other chewing or swallowing issues may become tired from chewing and leave their food. That is not good for them either. I suggest choosing food carefully, limit the total calories, and add more roughage, such as vegetables, to the diet, which will restrict calories. Some medications can make you gain weight, despite trying to control calories, so you should consider daily portions of cabbage, cauliflower, broccoli, or similar items, which makes the stomach full. You can keep the feeling of fullness and eat less while on these medications.

FASTING

We are not talking about religious fasting. Basically, this is skipping one meal per week, on any day you choose. Try not to eat either breakfast or lunch, and do not eat anything after the missed meal until the next day. Drink plenty of fluids. This type of limited fasting will not do any harm and does not deprive the brain of any necessary calories, oxygen, nutrients, or minerals. This is like giving the GI tract a rest. It is the same as giving the brain and mind a rest during sleep. It also rests the body, heart, and lungs while resting on a couch or bed. Remember, Buddha lived healthy and happy life, and he only ate one meal a day from age thirty-six to eighty-four. Fasting will also help to cleanse the GI tract and help the mind and brain to be more alert. This type of limited fasting will not cause any ketosis or hallucinations. Most people will have enough glucose stored in the liver to metabolize during the ten to twelve hours of fasting, but some may not tolerate fasting well. They will do okay by taking their medications as usual and keeping up with clear liquids.

Meaningful improvements in blood pressure, blood lipids, and biomarkers of oxidative stress can occur with no harm done. This will also assist in better digestion on a daily basis.

Do this once a week, and also try to skip an additional meal if you attend a party or have an extra large meal. This will help to balance the total calories for that day.

It is easier to give too much to the body, rather than taking away from it. The excess calories will accumulate quickly and are extremely difficult to get rid of. Each fasting day will help to mobilize a half pound of extra calories that are sitting in fatty deposits. Choose a day out of each week as a fasting day after lunch. This can be an automated reminder at the beginning of the week. Choose a day that is less demanding, so that you tolerate the fasting without anger and frustration from hunger. This can slowly become a routine habit. This will not develop into anorexia or bulimia unless you have obsessive tendencies for dieting and binging. You can take a multivitamin that day, but there is no real need with just one meal skipped per week.

Control excess calories and food intake as much as possible. Many dishes can make many diseases.

Bowel Cleansing

Some people, based on the nature of the food that they eat, their dietary habits, and their medical conditions, can become constipated or need to strain frequently. Consequences can include hemorrhoids and bleeding and abdominal discomfort. Meat lovers are more likely prone to this. Excessive laxative use can also cause habitual constipation.

It is necessary to drink plenty of fluids and eat plenty of fiber. Identify the foods that cause constipation and avoid them. Fruits are preferred, rather than juices. Still, if you are prone to constipation, add a stool softener to your daily medications.

If the problem continues after all medical reasons have been ruled out, try a limited dose of laxatives at intervals. Do not make it a habit. To avoid intolerance, try different laxatives, limiting their use to once or twice per month. Give the bowel a rest by fasting if possible, on alternate weeks. Despite all efforts, some GI tracts become stubborn, and autonomic dysfunction can result, which unfortunately can require frequent enemas.

Best Times to Eat

The maximum acid secretion in the stomach is from 10:00 p.m. to 2:00 a.m. It slowly rises again to reach its peak by 11:00 a.m. Correlating the two, the best time for food intake can be determined.

If there is no other medical condition that requires frequent eating or a need to eat each time with medication, follow these basic guidelines. It is preferable not to eat anything after eight o'clock until the next morning at nine o'clock. People often have a busy life, especially in the morning; they are often on the road by six or seven o'clock. Some people think they need to eat cereal for breakfast in the morning. This may not be a good idea. If you can take a small meal with you, wait to eat until nine o'clock. Eating brunch at eleven o'clock may be the right choice. Otherwise, eat a limited breakfast without juice. Fruit is okay as a substitute in the morning.

During lunch, avoid high fat/high calorie foods or smoothies. Once you're back at home after work, avoid snacking while sitting and relaxing. Also, use moderation and complete your dinner by six or seven o'clock. Try not to eat anything after eight o'clock.

As we discussed, you should be flexible with food, sometimes eating more, sometimes less. Based on what you have eaten, you can skip some meals without any problem and can compensate for a higher calorie intake.

Types of Foods that the Body and Brain Need

Eat Right and Reap the Benefits

Proteins, carbohydrates, fats, and water are the main building blocks of the body; they are needed on a daily basis in adequate proportions.

We get most of the vitamins and minerals we need on a daily basis through a balanced diet containing fruits, vegetables, proteins, carbohydrates, and fats.

Based on your health needs, you may need a multivitamin with minerals on a daily basis. You don't really need megavitamins. If you lack a certain vitamin, you can replace it with the proper dose. There are no tests that check each and every mineral or vitamin in the body for deficiencies, but your doctor can tell based on your symptoms. The following list contains some common vitamins and minerals that the body may need to replace when it is deficient.

Vitamin B12: Dietary intake is the only source for vitamin B12 (cyanocobalamin) and folic acid (folate) because we cannot synthesize them in the body.

People who eat a fair and balanced diet that includes vegetables can get enough of both, unless they have difficulty absorbing them through the stomach due to a lack of parietal cells. After age fifty, the GI tract loses the capability to absorb these vitamins, especially B12.

Pure vegetarians who drink only cow's milk can have low levels of B12. Cow's milk does not have any B12. Dietary supplementation of B12 is essential. Vitamin B12 can be supplemented in therapeutic or maintenance doses.

B12 deficiency can cause many symptoms, including depression, fatigue, memory loss, neuropathy, ataxia, lack of coordination, gait difficulty, disorientation, and spinal cord disease. Symptoms sometimes do not appear until two years after the deficiency. When blood levels show a deficiency, that means B12 has already depleted from the body and is ready to manifest into a clinical symptom or disease.

Recognizing this and treating it may help to some extent, but we will not be able to reverse it altogether if symptoms have already begun. Based on the deficiency, supplements should be maintained to prevent further ongoing damage to the brain, mind, body, and nervous system. B12 deficiency can contribute to dementia.

Folic acid: Pregnant women and people on different medications often require folic acid supplementation. Deficiency can lead to fatigue and depression. Folic acid is essential for normal brain functioning.

Blindly consuming megavitamins on a daily basis may not be a good idea, especially with vitamin A, vitamin D, vitamin E, and vitamin K, which can cause a problem called hypervitaminosis. It has its own consequences, with many different symptoms.

Vitamin B6 plays a role in the synthesis of serotonin, low levels of which is linked to depression. The various medications used as antidepressants are called selective serotonin receptor inhibitors (SSRIs). Vitamin B6 deficiency can also keep cells from absorbing oxygen from red blood cells. Based on the needs, this can be replaced. In older adults, the requirement may be higher.

Vitamin C is also essential as an antioxidant and for adequate brain functioning. It is especially beneficial for the elderly to take adequate amounts. Vitamin C is prevalent in all citrus fruits, and we get more than adequate amounts with a daily balanced diet.

Vitamin B2 is important in the body's production of energy. It's also needed for the proper functioning of vitamin B6. Often elderly people lack it, and daily multivitamin supplementation is probably necessary. Studies showed elderly people living alone consumed foods containing up to 25 percent less than the recommended daily intake of vitamin B2. Around 10 percent of them showed a deficiency.

Vitamin D: With people spending less and less time in the sun, and with the elderly staying indoors (mostly in nursing homes and assisted living facilities), we are not getting enough sun, causing a deficiency in vitamin D. This lack causes not only osteoporosis and weak bones, but cognitive issues as well, along with a higher risk for heart disease and some types of cancers. There are good evaluation methods and replacement therapies available. Vitamin D regulates the absorption and maintenance of normal calcium levels in the bloodstream.

Vitamin K: Usually, we do not need this as a separate supplement. All green leafy vegetables have this in adequate amounts. People who are on Coumadin (Warfarin), a blood thinner, need to take some precautions regarding excess intake of vitamin K. Your doctor can advise you regarding the types of vegetables to consume if you take Coumadin.

MINERALS

A balanced diet provides adequate amounts of micronutrients and minerals. that include selenium, zinc, chromium, nickel, copper, calcium, and iron, magnesium, calcium, sodium (in the form of salt), and potassium. Doctors can help to guide your requirements for sodium and potassium based on your health conditions and the medications you may be on. Minerals like magnesium can get low because of decreased absorption from the GI track. Magnesium is necessary in the body's production of energy. Based on need, your doctor could replace it rather than have you take magnesium-containing supplements, which can harm patients with kidney disease. Too much magnesium in the body can cause problems if the kidneys cannot remove it.

A deficiency in iron causes anemia. There are blood tests available to confirm iron deficiency, and it is easily treated with supplements. Women who are pregnant or who lose a lot of blood during their menstrual cycles commonly get deficient in iron and need replacement therapy.

Copper is linked to both psychiatric and brain disorders, especially Wilson's disease, which causes neuropsychiatric problems. It plays a major role in the functioning of serotonin. It is also important in maintaining proper brain function and energy production. It also helps in the synthesis of myelin, a nerve cell sheath. This is different from demyelination, which causes multiple sclerosis. There are adequate testing methods to treat copper deficiency, rather than taking megavitamins.

Remember, a balanced diet should have most of what you need. Based on what you need, specific deficiencies can be replaced rather than blindly taking megavitamins or other minerals. Vitamins in excess quantities can cause hypervitaminosis. Another issue is that the liver or kidneys cannot handle too much minerals. Again, moderation is the key term here to practice.

A Few Words on Spices and Neurology

Dark chocolate has flavonoids that help to improve memory.

Turmeric, garlic, and ginger are useful for many reasons and have been in use for millennia. No harm noted and no calories.

Sprinkle a few grams of turmeric on any food, just like salt (maximum ten to twelve grams). Turmeric contains curcumin, a chemical that helps memory and pain relief. While research continues for its uses in treating Alzheimer's, no adverse effects were noted with daily usage as a food additive. Turmeric may help the immune system retain memory. It is widely available as a powder and can be found in any food store.

Garlic: There are many well-known benefits of garlic, and it is available in many forms. Fresh garlic can be used in dishes on a daily basis. There is a slight smell when excreted through sweat. Some people cannot take the smell. It has benefits for both neurological and cardiac health.

Ginger is available fresh or as a dry powder. It can be used in any dish, just like black pepper. Fresh ginger is spicy. It is thought to be good for memory; it may cut down chronic pain, migraines, and fibromyalgia-related pain as well.

Green tea: Recent research indicates green tea can protect against Alzheimer's disease with its antioxidant effects and by reducing plaque formation in the brain.

Food Plate (choosemyplate.gov)

We Are Getting Everything that We Need

If we follow the food plate/food pyramid recommendations, we will get everything that we need, with supplements as needed; most people can take a multivitamin on a daily basis. One can consume alcohol in moderation. This is an optional recommendation, not for everyone. Also, there is no reason to drink alcohol. But if you like it and enjoy it, it is fine; again, moderation is the key while consuming.

You should eat sparingly red meat, processed meat, butter, refined grains, white rice, bread, pasta, and potatoes sparingly, and limit sugary drinks, sweets, and salt.

Consume healthy fats and oils like olive oil. Extra-virgin olive oil is the best, and canola, soy, corn, sunflower oils are okay. Use peanut oil sparingly.

Whole grains, brown rice, whole wheat, and oats are preferred. You should have five to seven servings per day of healthy fats like nuts, seeds, olive oil, soy foods, and avocados. Fish is preferred; the best is coldwater fish like trout and salmon.

You should only have two to six servings of fish and seafood per week. Beans and legumes are rich in magnesium, potassium, soluble fiber, and folic acid. Nontropical fruits are rich in antioxidants. Bananas and citrus fruits are a natural source of potassium.

Pure Vegans will find some items from above list as not their choices.

ANCILLARY FOOD ITEMS (NOT REQUIRED, BUT COMMONLY USED)

Addiction: Some substances create euphoria and subsequently make you crave them. Even Sigmund Freud was not immune. This one of the fathers of psychiatry fell victim to cocaine while trying to learn its capabilities. He had to work so hard to get back to himself from its destruction.

Caffeine

This substance does not contain any essential nutrients. The human body does not require caffeine, but most people use it. Some people are almost dependent on it on a daily basis to function. Suddenly stopping caffeine intake can cause headaches, lack of concentration, and mood swings, and you may not be able to perform at work or manage job efficiently.

Do we need caffeine on a daily basis? The answer is no. It can help as a headache medication. People use it to stay awake, which is also a manufactured symptom due to their erratic sleeping habits and hectic schedules.

To recover from sleep deprivation, one needs to sleep. To stay awake or to finish the job, people opt for caffeinated beverages or other stimulants.

Overall, caffeine is not a dangerous substance as long as it is used in limited proportions, as long as the user can tolerate it with no heart rhythm issues, like tachycardia, or stomach issues, like ulcers, which can get worse with caffeine.

If there are no other medical conditions, limited intake of caffeine is okay. You should avoid drinking caffeine after midday, especially for people who prefer to be asleep by ten o'clock.

If someone works the night shift and tries to stay awake by drinking caffeinated beverages, they should stay away from caffeine during the daytime.

Here are some beverages with caffeine content:

- Brewed coffee: 100–150 mg/cup

- Instant coffee: 85–100 mg/cup

- Tea: 60–75 mg/cup

- Cola: 40–60 mg/cup

Decaffeinated coffee is not free of caffeine. It still contains up to one-fifth the caffeine of regular coffee.

The over-the-counter medications that people use for headaches have up to 100 mg of caffeine per tablet.

Alcohol

The food plate/food pyramid recommends alcohol as optional with discretion, I believe alcohol is not needed and is not a food item either. In all possible ways, it should be avoided. People who claim to drink wine for health purposes should be careful not to exceed the limit and try not to make it into a habit.

In fact, alcohol is the number one item causing harm to users in all possible ways, as per the UK *Drug Harms Report,* a multicriteria analysis study by David Nutt, a British psychiatrist and pharmacologist. After alcohol were heroin, crack cocaine, methamphetamines, cocaine, tobacco, amphetamines, and marijuana. In November 2010, Nutt wrote an article on the study, published in *The Lancet* and coauthored with Les King and Lawrence Phillips.

There is a link with alcohol abuse and genetics. Children of alcoholics are four times more likely to become alcoholics or become depressed. Sons are affected more than daughters. Around 1 out of 10 adults are alcohol dependent. Alcohol is known to reduce the life span as much as ten years. Females absorb alcohol faster, and it quickly reaches peak blood levels.

Meanwhile, if people prefer to drink for health purposes and there are no contraindications, they should have no more than two beers per day (for an average built male); females are recommended to have only one beer per day.

But be careful with the medications that you are on. Some can interfere with alcohol, so check with your physician.

If you are trying different alcoholic beverages, containing different proportions of alcohol by percentage, be prudent and limit your intake to match one or two beers of total alcohol content per day.

People with migraine headaches may who want to drink an alcoholic beverage. If they cannot tolerate other drinks, they can try a small amount of vodka; somehow, it is well tolerated in most migraine patients without causing an acute headache.

People with psychiatric and neurological conditions should consult their physician regarding alcohol intake and interactions with medications or derailment of the neurological status.

Knowing its harmful effects, we have used alcohol for centuries. It may be useful for some cardiac issues or certain tremors, but it is not advised to gravitate toward it.

Shakespeare said that alcohol "provokes the desire, but it takes away the performance."

Drunkenness is the failure of a man to control his thoughts.—David Grayson

F. Scott Fitzgerald (September 24, 1896–December 21, 1940), a famous American author, had been an alcoholic since his college days. He became notorious during the 1920s for his heavy drinking, leaving him in poor health by the late 1930s. He is widely regarded as one of the greatest American writers of the twentieth century. Fitzgerald finished four novels: *This Side of Paradise, The Beautiful and Damned, Tender Is the Night,* and his most famous, *The Great Gatsby.* A fifth, unfinished novel, *The Love of the Last Tycoon,* was published posthumously. Fitzgerald also wrote many short stories that treated themes of youth and promise along with despair and age. He died at age forty-four. (wikipedia)

Marijuana

Today, marijuana is a popular substance, used in both recreationally and medicinally. People use marijuana medically to relieve pain and nausea, especially by patients with cancer and chronic pain. It is also widely available for recreational purposes, especially among the younger generation. Some doctors feel it has only limited purpose in pain management. Like tobacco and alcohol, I believe there is no general purpose for its routine use.

Chronic use may worsen a patient's depression, which is something we see quite commonly in the hospital. Users often come back with worse depression, panic reactions, impaired judgment, and an altered mental state.

Some patients complain of dizziness, headaches, and blood pressure issues. The long-term negative side effects of using marijuana is not known, but a lot of research is ongoing. Recent reports show that close to 50 percent of Americans wanted to see marijuana legalized.

Marijuana causes Amotivational syndrome in long-term users, resulting in loss of desire to function.

Tobacco

Albert Einstein was a heavy smoker. I advise my patients to stay away from it. If you smoke, please quit as soon as possible using your willpower. There are harmful effects to yourself, to your loved ones, and to society.

There is no correlation between gender and the success rate for quitting smoking. The ability to quit depends on your desire to give up the addiction and how comfortable you believe the process will be.

Nicotine and tobacco has been shown to help Alzheimer's disease and memory to some extent. But due to the health hazards of smoking, you should stay away from tobacco. Not everyone who smokes gets every side effect. It is not predictable. It affects the body in many ways over time: blue puffers (people with emphysema) and pink bloaters (people with asthma), rough skin on the face, and coarse voice.

Unusual Complaints and Symptoms with Common Food

Food allergies: Many people are allergic to foods; if you become allergic to any new food, you should avoid it. Gluten sensitivity, lactose intolerance, and other food-related sensitivities are beyond the scope of this book.

Reveal is limited to briefings on diet regarding brain and mind needs, but I will present a few unusual symptoms here. If you are facing these issues, please contact your doctor.

Salt

Salt intake should be limited, especially if you have relevant health conditions. No one needs excess salt, unless they lose it due to heavy sweating, like athletes or people who work in the sun. If you crave salt, please see your doctor to make sure you don't have an adrenal gland problem like Addison's disease or other medical causes. An unusual craving for highly salty foods is one symptom to watch for.

Other Symptoms

Eating in moderation is most important. Most of us eat more than we need, consuming more calories. But if you fear eating, after psychiatric causes (including anorexia nervosa) are eliminated, you should be evaluated to rule out any GI track issues. Mesenteric ischemia causes particular pain in the epigastric region, which begins shortly after eating. Symptoms usually start half an hour to one hour after eating and can last a few hours. This makes people develop a fear of eating or an aversion for foods, and they start losing weight.

If you develop headaches after a protein-rich meal, you may have Ornithine transcarbamylase deficiency. This typically involves migraines, nausea, vomiting, lethargy, and confusion. These headaches can be extremely severe. Testing can be done and treatments are available, including limiting dietary protein.

If you get headaches with palpitations and sweating during urination, it may be due to a tumor of the urinary bladder that secretes catecholamines called pheochromocytoma. This can cause high blood pressure too.

Sometimes, headaches occur during an orgasm; tests should be run to rule out leaking aneurysms or bleeding in the brain.

Laughter is a sign of good health, happiness, and a good mood;

it can keep you healthy. However, if you laugh at inappropriate times, psychiatric conditions should be ruled out. The possibility of brain diseases should also be considered and evaluated. Strokes and diseases like multiple sclerosis and ALS (Lou Gehrig's disease) can cause emotional lability and inappropriate laughter (or crying). Your doctor can evaluate you, but there are not many treatments available yet.

While smoking is not recommended, some smokers develop a sudden aversion to the taste for cigarettes; this may be due to acute viral hepatitis, which is easily tested for.

I also do not recommend alcohol consumption, even in moderation, but sometimes people develop pain after drinking alcohol; they are advised to see their doctor to rule out Hodgkin's lymphoma. Many other cancers (head, neck, throat, breast, uterus, cervical, and bladder cancers) can cause this uncommon symptom. Pancreatitis can cause similar complaints. This can proceed months or even years before the diagnosis of cancer is made. Treatment includes avoiding alcohol; consult your physician for further management.

Ice: Many people like to chew or eat large amounts of ice with beverages: this craving for ice may be due to an iron deficiency; anemia can be from various causes, including monthly menstrual loss in females. Treating the iron loss and anemia should overcome the craving for ice.

Water: People should drink plenty of water. Those with congestive heart failure, liver failure, renal failure, and other conditions may need to limit their fluid intake based on their doctor's recommendations. If you have an intense thirst, see your doctor to rule out diabetes insipidus. This is different from Type I and

Type II diabetes, which is due to insulin deficiency. Diabetes insipidus is cause by brain- or kidney-related difficulties; the lack of a hormone called vasopressin in the brain can keep the kidneys from functioning properly. This leads to enhanced water loss from the kidneys, causing a craving for water. Please see your doctor, because people on certain medications can also develop this problem.

The tongue is a vital organ; it enables us to taste, chew, and swallow. It is also the main organ for the articulation of speech. If you have pain in the tongue while chewing food, see your doctor to rule out cancer and other problems, such as poor blood supply to the tongue due to atherosclerosis or temporal arteritis (inflamed arteries).

UNCOMMON TOLERANCES

Many pain issues are based on our tolerance for pain as well as conditioning and cultural and emotional issues. Extreme pain can lead to several consequences, such as hyperalgesia and hypoalgesia (more sensitivity and less sensitivity to pain).

Recently, I saw two patients having these extremes. One morning in the urgent care area, a construction worker in his twenties was brought in with his fingertip bleeding. He did not express any pain. The staff put him in a room, and while making him ready for cauterization to stop the bleeding, he refused any pain medicine. I cauterized his finger with an electric needle. It caused a burning smell, but he was calm, quiet, and showed no discomfort. He came back for checkups but never asked for pain medication.

Two days later, a young woman came in with her boyfriend,

crying, screaming, and jumping around in pain. She had cut her fingertip while chopping vegetables in the kitchen.

When I looked at the cut, I was surprised. It was an extremely tiny, superficial laceration on the tip of the finger. She did not need any stitches or pain meds, just a band-aid. I discharged her with no concerns.

These are two extreme examples of pain tolerance.

Part 3

Rebuild Yourself

Twenty years from now, you will be more disappointed by the things that you did not do than by the ones you did so. So throw off the bowlines. Sail away from the safe harbor. Catch the trade winds in your sails. Explore, dream, discover the challenge, the joy of growth.—Mark Twain

Let us all try to evolve from the conscious and subconscious minds into a superconscious mind, with the constant evolution of perfect thoughts, feelings, and hope to see through the eyes of our souls.

Until now, if it was not your option, it could be yours now. Your goals do not have a deadline.

You can bring the self behind yourself, and the subconscious mind behind your conscious mind.

Cognitive reconstruction will lead you to a new person and will make you what you wanted to be. The sparks of positive forces within want to become yours and drive away the negative forces.

The subconscious mind will exist no more; alone, it cannot force you to take any wrong turns or make wrong decisions.

Stream of thought, one by one, continuously trying to influence you to go back to your old self, which is full of negative forces. Only consistent good practice will keep you from going back to them.

That is the way we are designed. So we have to work hard to keep up with positive thoughts and to keep the negative forces away from us for long-term benefits.

Until now, your negative stream of thoughts made your own energy the enemy. Your own thoughts favored the negative thoughts in the form of wasting your potential with excessive worry and giving importance to the unwanted, unproductive thoughts storming your brain. They are filling your thinking process and memory cells.

This self-designed course in meditation will help bring out your motivation. It helps to control the way mental energy is focused and trained. Also, it helps to spend time on positive motives and utilize your capabilities to rise above and show the real potential inside. This obsessive but focused training of your mind will bring harmony and stop the streaming thoughts to make your real personality prevail.

Just like a well-built dam can irrigate the soil and help generate electric power, your well-oriented thoughts will make you flourish with new joy and clarity of vision, and make you more productive and ambitious. You will enjoy work just for the work's sake, and results will come without asking or looking for them.

The theory of energy, says that "energy can be changed from one form into another form" but mental energy behaves differently. Once idle and not goal oriented, it is not neutral anymore. It always prefers negative thoughts and self-destruction. When you start using it in a negative way, it magnifies that energy many times; it not only destroys inner harmony, it also makes the people around you or those who depend on you miserable. So the only way mental energy should flow is for a positive interest and improvement. The pain of suffering, worry, failure, inadequacy, and self-pity needs to be known to every mind, so everyone can experience the opposite of it. This will help us to see what is there on the other side.

At this time, you already know the suboptimal nature. You have to look forward and hope not to experience the worrisome face again. The unlimited potential that you have will take this whole life to reap the rewards and enjoy the real joy in it. A wise person said, "If this life is not enough to experience all the happiness and joy itself, then where is the time to worry?"

For enlightened people, there is no worry or sadness. They experience the balance or homeostasis so that everything is a balanced joy. We need to adapt to the daily tides of life and emotions. We require additional training to face the worries and make them into less energy-spending tasks without causing mental fatigue. This will enable us to continue to the next day and the next venture with peace and joy. Life is dynamic, with daily emotional and ego clashes that keep the mind from resting, just like the heart has to beat all the time. Imagine during sleep, especially quiet sleep, the calm mind gives rest to the heart and the whole body. That is why we have a slow heart rate during sleep. So the vital act of resting your mind is the key to overall bodily joy and health.

First, please be aware of the common features of your personality. If they include sudden outbursts of emotions, know that this happens, not because you are holding them for a long time, but because your mind is filled with unnecessary thoughts that are inappropriate. Then outbursts of temper, rage, and anger come out of you. This not only causes a destructive force to the current situation, it also pushes you back in the process of self-realization, causing despair that you may never change. With firm training, you can contain and minimize future outbursts.

Even though you love your family and your children, you may routinely show emotional outbursts toward them. The incidents of the day or your own never-ending worries may exhaust your mind, and your dear ones will get the toll of your anger. Until you eliminate subconscious anger, worry, and resentment by conscious efforts with prolonged self-disciplined training, you cannot come out of that vicious cycle.

I met with one family that endured these types of incidents. The man was quiet and emotionally balanced, hard-working and financially successful. However, he repeatedly lost his temper with his children and wife after coming home from work. This man loved his family and lived for them, so why was this happening? The answer was, he needed further homeostasis of his mind. He did not find the proper outlet for his outbursts. He chose his family for that, subconsciously or unconsciously, just like drinking a beer or taking a nap to relax his mind. But indirectly, he made the family unhappy, despite giving them everything. Instead of that, he should have tried to eliminate his emotional outbursts. Anyone can do this with further practice. Even at the end of a long day, mental fatigue will not build up with consistent practice. We may blame being overworked and fatigued. But it is not true if the mind is not fatigued. The mind will not get fatigued as long as we maintain homeostasis.

You don't need an alcoholic beverage to rest your mind; the practice of meditation will do it. The immense joy and potential the trained mind can create is limitless. Life is for living in harmony. First, you need to establish harmony within yourself, and it will automatically be established amongst your fellow humans, animals, nature, and the universe. Then you will see that mighty power everywhere, not only as mental strength but pervading everything and rejuvenating everything. You need not repress or deny anger or misjudge anything. Everything will flow, in a well-established way, in front of your conscious mind to choose and guide the best feeling for you. The best actions and results will follow. No more self-pity, and the conscious mind will be aware and be able to deal with things constructively. You will not give away yourself to those destructive feelings if you are constantly on alert and train your mind. Obsessive training is for self knowledge only, and that builds your own new self. You have to be frank and honest with yourself to see what is causing all this disturbance.

RULES OF PRACTICE, STEP 1

Acknowledge all your positive (constructive) and negative (destructive) feelings.

Be firm in the effort to change the negative attitudes and enhance the positive attitudes that you already have.

Be obsessive to acquire and learn new things that you potentially can accommodate.

Promise yourself that you will be totally frank and transparent with yourself, and never give up the practice.

Prepare for years and years of practice to attain homeostasis of your mental energy.

By following these rules for yourself, you will see the change in a positive way. You will feel so much relief and be able to calm your emotional streaming. You will feel like the master of your mind.

That feeling will certainly motivate you to pursue a permanent change. In the process, don't take the destructive thoughts and feelings too seriously; don't feel overwhelmed with positive emotions either. Even if you can't eliminate them and become free of distressing feelings or thoughts, your goal is to let them go consciously, just like you are watching without being involved in it, so that the emotions do not stay with you and drain your energy further. This will help you to slowly gain the benefit of conscious choice and show you how to act and react to a particular situation.

RULES OF PRACTICE, STEP 2

Never give up until you achieve the purpose.

Recall your goals repeatedly if you feel like giving up.

Say loudly to yourself, "I will succeed and will not give up in this new self-making."

Nothing is more urgent and valuable than making your new self.

At the beginning, any attempt to repress negative emotions will only increase their intensity and make the situation worse, but do not give up. Momentarily give up and let that emotion pass with no obstacles consciously, but do not act on it.

Restrain or resist the negative destructive feelings that weaken your mind and personality. Hold them in check. Do not let them damage or disturb your aims or ambitions; continue to maintain balance of mind.

THE SEVEN-DAY FORMULA

To stop destructive emotions, consciously postpone an issue for seven days. This will automatically dilute the emotional content and anger, so clarity of thinking on that particular issue will prevail. The same issue will not look worse if you don't act with spontaneous emotions.

THE THREE-POINT FORMULA

Minor issues associated with anger can be dissipated with this process.

Stay calm.

Look calm.

Plan alternative measures to a spontaneous reaction.

This can be done before resentment develops further.

Always allow feelings to flow freely. If you perceive subconscious feelings through your conscious mind, like a spectator, you can stop the stream of destructive negative feelings and change them into a positive force.

When your subconscious mind is functioning (not for severely demented persons), you cannot obliterate emotional forces by any means, but you can channel them properly, convince them to disappear faster, and change them into positive ones with no cause to indulge. This will strengthen the self with more motivation, aims, and goals.

Just like a flooding river's destruction can be stopped by thoughtfully designing a dam, the enormous mental energy that is consumed by negative feelings of a self-destructive nature, like anger, fear, hatred, grudge, rumination, resentment, and jealousy, can be conserved for valuable thought processes.

The idle brain consumes more energy than an active brain, if not in harmony while idle.

Negative thoughts and emotions consume enormous energy compared to pleasurable and positive constructive thoughts.

So a person suffering and experiencing obsessive, vicious cycles of negative thought processes and self-pity needs more time to recoup mental fatigue.

Just like a dying battery does not last long, a negatively charged emotional brain fatigues faster and has less physical energy available to respond to stimuli when needed. You may get aches and pains, joint soreness, stiffness, heavy breathing, frequent yawning, and a foggy brain as a physical consequence.

Everything is told everywhere and in countless generations, but we have got plenty of time to practice.

Everything we can achieve right from this point, all our potential, can be unrevealed.

Buddha tightened his mind and released it when needed. He mostly followed the middle way of practice after enlightenment. He never thought of giving up his quest for enlightenment, despite facing extreme weather and hunger. He never thought of going back to his comfortable way of life in the palace by giving up his quest for enlightenment. He never let his worries bother him, but he let them go. Once he adopted the middle way, he followed it the rest of his life; he analyzed each situation without negligence or overindulgence, and he took steps to remedy each situation by never losing sight of truth and righteousness. You can achieve that middle way of Buddha. He was extremely confident of what he was doing, and we all agree the truth remains forever. You can practice it from where you are now, and using all his teachings and wisdom, you can practice until you achieve enlightenment.

Paucity and adversity are our teachers. They teach us how to develop courage, wisdom, and self-control to deal with our problems, so we come out with joy by shedding our worries. Until we develop those traits, we need to learn from adversity and insufficiency, which can remind us of what we need. Once we get what we need, the teachings will remain with us forever. For us to acquire that, we need practice, practice, and practice. We must practice until we acquire. We will aspire and dream about everything in the way of truth and righteousness.

There Is No Alternative to Meditation

Buddha practiced it, even in his last minute of nirvana. It is not easy to meditate in the real sense. The world itself is both serene and scary. To stay in emptiness is rare and difficult. Meditating for two hours, like Buddha, is hard; meditating for just thirty minutes, or even one minute, is impossible for many of us, despite practice.

We can make a boat stand still in the stormy ocean, but we cannot empty our mind. By trying different ways of practicing meditation, we can do better with most of our mental struggles and unrest.

If everything follows Buddha's middle way, why not meditation? You need not practice strict rules. You do not even need to sit up in the lotus position or practice at a particular time. You can do this as contemplation and concentrate on a good thought while driving, watching TV, showering, in bed, day or night. The only thing you have to do is think about or recall good thoughts and memories and let the worries leave.

Your ocean of thoughts will slowly become less stormy; your mind will become more stable. Just like your vision is improved by clearing the fog, you can see the shore better; your thoughts will be crisper and can approach the goals awaiting you. Your further journey will be more energetic and vibrant and enthusiastic; your mind will be clear.

I promise, once you see your calm mind, you will want to maintain it with more practice, and ultimately you will find meditation becomes closer to you, and it will remain with you as it did with Buddha. For that, you have to think like Buddha. He used to think like an archer who curiously investigated the length of his arrow, the strength of his arm, his aim, and his release; when he hit the target unexpectedly, he became the Buddha, who went into meditation for a few hours spontaneously during his childhood.

Is it possible for everyone? Among the world's seven billion humans and countless new souls, only a few out of many generations probably can achieve enlightenment. But what about the rest of us? Most of us belong to Buddha's two types of fools, which are

the fool who knows he is a fool, and

the fool who considers himself a wise man.

Buddha himself took six years of practice and self-enquiry to achieve enlightenment.

The second category, being what they are, also suffer from streaming thoughts from second to second, movement to movement, jumping from good to bad, love to hate, judging to nonjudging, balance to imbalance, emotions, anger, joy, pity, and self doubt. In these movements, you lose your self and live those negative follies to develop grudges that lead to destruction of self and others. You lose your courage, wisdom, self-confidence, and balance of intellect and mind, with your soul weeping forever.

The swinging of the mind between good and bad follies, with recouping in the next minute, with exhaustion of mind and thoughts well shaken with frustration, are awaiting to repeat and again. How long can the agony last? Meanwhile, the losses are growing with emotional imbalance. How many countless times? It will never end for real. In this impermanent life, with intact mind and either healthy or unhealthy physical body until the last breath, they are all part of us. Just as Buddha said, "They come and go, they pass away." Even a fool with the guidance of a master can change to a greater extent, with continuous practice. We are not trying to extinguish all the feelings that are flowing like a never-ending river. The nonstop buzzing sounds of follies and emotions in our mind cause suffering to our heart and soul. If our existence is suffering, can we turn it to joy and contentment? We want to learn how to make those streams of thoughts go away and make less frequent visits yet leave us quickly. While going away, just like the river makes a fertile delta or a train takes on more passengers from station to station, let our good thoughts enrich our mind with courage, wisdom, confidence, and compassion to grow further in our lives toward success and joy.

Most of us have wisdom, but we lose it due to circumstances. Here and there, we do see the wisdom in us, now and then covered under the daily routines of life's emotions, which are dominated by ignorance. First we have to accept and acknowledge our own good emotions and thoughts within us.

Just like you can see a small fetus grow for nine months, with good prenatal care, and be born and grow well with good care and nourishment from loving parents, let your wisdom's seed grow further, with your awareness and consciousness to recognize it. Let it take time. It may not be immediately possible, with your demanding life styles and needs. But once you acknowledge it, you have seen the bliss of wisdom already. You can trace it and nurture it to grow further. You can say good-bye to your negative emotions one by one. While doing so, you must be prepared to tolerate the back-and-forth swings of suffering and worries. First, you can use it for your own joy and help, and then the overflow of goodness can spontaneously help others, and you can contribute to the whole universe, to all forms of life. For that, first you have to help yourself to come out of your thoughts of worry and embrace the good thoughts of wisdom with practice.

Not only the success, but the struggle to reach success is also a pleasure and part of the outcome of success.

Let us struggle now; we can enjoy both the struggle and success. We are all impermanent in these bodies; all of us know that.

Everyone wants to live; none of us want to die.—Buddha

We might prolong our existence with current medical advancements that even Buddha would have accepted to alleviate pain and suffering and prolong a healthy existence. Knowing that our last breath is inevitable, even with a prolonged life, let us make our minds a strong castle to reach that final minute's last breath with peace and in a painless state.

Let our mind gain and enjoy the wisdom in our life for our own betterment and use that wisdom in the last movement of life to take that deep breath with a smile of contentment; make that last breath the nirvana. Let it go. The past is past.

BEGINNING

First, be yourself. There is nothing wrong with that.

Analyze all your positive and negative forces within yourself.

Chart them down, and make a priority list.

Chart out a plan to eliminate some forces and assimilate others.

Prepare to say good-bye to past experiences; they are truly from the past, and they keep coming back into your memory and causing unpleasantness.

They are outdated or expired thoughts or events and have no constructive role in the present.

Ignore anything that is not supporting your conscious aims toward your planned goals. Let them dry up from your mind slowly with practice.

Each time they try to surface in your thoughts, tell them to go. You are interested only in positive forces, which you will invite to stay with you.

It takes a lot of practice to bring two minds together in harmony. It takes time to make ceaseless conscious efforts with the subconscious mind to work together for the common good and to keep your subconscious mind from summoning the negative forces. You are making the effort confidently, firmly, without begging your subconscious mind and without surrendering to it. Your practice will help you to do so.

With that much determined now, you have to choose your targets and goals.

You need to remove invalid goals, those that became a habit to the subconscious mind, and toss them from your conscious actions.

Choose the priority changes that you want to implement as part of your new goals.

Set an arbitrary time frame to reach these goals, but as is said, "Not too tight or too loose."

It starts with a simple step-by-step approach, as long as you don't give up your efforts and conscious thoughts for change.

So far, you've decided to change and acquire positive forces and stabilize them. You also chose a priority list and decided which to use first and which one is next. Now plan to practice consistently.

Frustration is common in any practice. Try to relax and take adequate steps to relieve it and get back to your practice again. When you leave frustration unattended, it will turn into laziness, and the purpose gets ignored.

Our greatest glory is not in never falling but in rising every time we fall.—Confucius

Visualize changes with imagination. Life has more dreams and imagination than sleep. Imagining and wishing are not enough, but they help keep your goals alive, keeps them in the limelight, so your practice and persistence will make them a reality. In this process, think about your past efforts and subsequent failures.

Maybe there were some misguided, miscalculated, but well-intended efforts and motives. Maybe some defects and obstacles made your efforts fail. Correct them this time. If wrong again, you are prepared to make more corrections, but giving up is not an option this time. Do not use avoidance tactics; you are going to face them correctly.

Remember, a good life is made up of a lot of sacrifices, either big or small. They include a lot of compromise and effort.

The brain and mind need harmonious efforts to keep the negative forces away, to chase them down and get rid of them with continuous practice. One after another, like a stream, negative forces flow in the mind. Show your will power against all the odds to work for success and peace.

Remember, no one has ever lived without struggles, without facing issues and problems. No one has survived without trembling thoughts, actions, loss, or compromise, and we are not different. We have to face the same yin-yang (50/50).

Go to bed regularly as per your sleep needs, preferably around 10:30 p.m., wake up around 6:30 a.m. In the morning, sit quietly in bed for ten minutes and try to meditate. Then get up out of bed and stretch your spine and all your muscles: neck, hips, shoulders, and arms.

Take one day at a time.

Before starting today's meditation, say to yourself, "I have a long way to go; with practice, I will not give up. I am prepared. I have plenty of potential and will try my level best with patience."

Knowledge of what is possible is the beginning of happiness.—George Santayana

Tell yourself the following:

"I will control my anger, despair, and hopeless feelings."

"I will control my obsessive, compulsive thoughts of rumination on negative things that are pulling me down."

"I will think only forward; I will not go back to past ruminations; I will worry less over past events."

"I will concentrate only on positive aspects to prop up during my meditation."

"I will leave all egos here. I am happy with my achievements so far and have the confidence to carry out more tasks and reach better goals."

While meditating, if your mind wanders, let it wander with the stream of thoughts. At the beginning, it is still okay to do so.

Eventually, with the persistence of practice, it will return and stay in its place. Then you will slowly start feeling the emptiness by itself.

Mindfulness is the by-product of that emptiness. Each bit of mindfulness takes you deeper into the meditation of a conscious nature. This keeps you away from worries, sadness, anxiety, and obsessiveness. And your compulsive, impulsive behaviors will improve. Your concentration and the ability of your brain to function better will improve. Your brain and your mind's abilities will improve as well.

Sit up or recline comfortably. It is okay to sit down in a comfortable position or lay down comfortably too.

SOME RECOMMENDATIONS

If you can't get into a typical sitting posture due to your health condition, then sit down in a comfortable position. If you prefer to lay down, do so comfortably. Either rest your head against the headboard of the bed or lay down on a pillow, with your arms resting on your chest like in a sleeping position. Slowly relax your muscles, and take a deep breath. Hold your breath as long as you can. Make sure your health condition permits it. Holding your breath may not be a good idea if you have congestive heart failure, COPD, asthma, or similar limitations.

You must be more alive and alert in the state of meditation. Release your breath, and take one or two normal breaths. Then again, take a deep breath and hold it as long as you can. This raises your concentration ability and calms down your mind to keep it in place by slightly raising the concentration of carbon dioxide in your blood, so people with any related health issues should not hold their breath; they can take normal breaths and continue meditation exercises.

Typically, meditating people concentrate by closing their eyes, but look in between the eyes or the area above the nose between eyebrows, which is called the Glabella. If you cannot do that, there are three other ways to concentrate.

Sit down in a quiet area while meditating and listen to the faint pulsating sound in your ears. If you cannot do that, try to concentrate and listen to your own heart beat while you're taking your breath and releasing it. If you cannot do that, imagine a bright dot with your eyes closed and concentrate on it.

Once you practice and are able to sustain this, slowly turn your mind into goal-oriented exercise.

If your mind wanders for a while, let it be. There is no need to sit down in one particular meditation posture. Remember, meditation is a brain exercise, not a body exercise at this point. People with disabilities, neurological conditions, or degenerative arthritis, even younger people with sports injuries or other issues, cannot maintain a sitting posture comfortably. That can destroy the whole concept of brain training and meditation. So find a comfortable position to do your meditation, not just one strict posture.

Start slowly, taking a deep breath, and hold it as long as you can. Let your mind slowly release its hold on negative thoughts, and let it dive deeper, setting harmony with your subconscious mind. Now both the conscious and subconscious minds are bound together. Now you can control your mind with your will power, as they are together in harmony.

Exhale slowly.

Recall your goals once again.

Take another deep breath, hold it, and release.

Slowly your mind will come back to its place.

Do subconscious conversation about your goals.

Continue this for thirty minutes to an hour on a daily basis.

**To climb steep hills requires slow
pace at first.—Shakespeare**

Look back and reflect on changes every day before you start
your next meditation session. It is like climbing a spiral staircase.
You feel like you're still where you started, but you are climbing.
The same way at the beginning; you don't see the results in the
geometric proportion, but after each day of determination and
practice, subconsciously you are making progress, and it will show
up as a permanent change later; as long as you don't give up, you
will be the winner at the end.

Discover the power inside you. Unlock it and determine to pursue
happiness and success. Don't go back in time. Think only forward
and see what you could change. Don't let your mood and emotions
hold you back.

Ask yourself consciously, in the morning and a few more times
during the day, about the following:

- What is on my mind?

- How does my body feel?

- What are my goals for today?

- How do I feel overall?

This self-inquiry will slowly become a day-to-day planner. This reminds you of your own state of mind, keeps your thoughts from drifting toward worries and negative thoughts, and keeps you goal oriented.

We are still masters of our own fate. We are still captains of our own souls.—Winston Churchill

PRACTICE: TO CULTIVATE A QUESTING MIND

Think about the goal.

Sit down and relax (or lie down comfortably).

Breathe in and out easily.

Tell every part of your body, including your muscles, to relax.

Breathe in and out, forgetting your worries.

Practice this until your mind becomes calm and empty.

Write down some positive phrases that you like and repeat them in the morning and later during your daily routine.

Also write down the things that bother you most. This helps you to identify your worries and negative aspects of your mind.

Tell yourself repeatedly that you are working on them and that you're going to get rid of those worries soon (self-talk).

Postpone the worries for the time being.

Pay more attention to some positive activity.

Always keep your self-confidence.

Frustration and despair may come during your activities. Take them without bodily expression of any destructive urge. Let them pass, but look calm and composed. Feel comfort in what you do; always prepare to work just for work's sake, not looking for a selfish motive.

Once you come to this stage of planning, you are ready to give a sincere trial and are ready to plan a week of activity of positive attitude with definite tasks each day. So prepare yourself and determine to carry out that weekly activity.

Imagine yourself, project yourself in that activity. At the end of each day, review your efforts and activities.

This will help to consolidate your mind energy to focus on positive aspects and to break the bad habits or routines that your mind wants to continue. This helps you to concentrate on your goal, prepares you to face your problems with determination, and gives you courage for further planning.

Now analyze yourself and find the waste pipes of energy that are dumping all your meaningful thoughts.

Deal with each thought carefully. Be frank with yourself first; successfully eliminate each waste pipe that is making your thoughts go the wrong path. Remember, we create ourselves constantly as we go along.

From your own estimate of capabilities and set of your own targets, you define yourself.

Develop multiple channels for self-expression.

Eliminate all your negative thoughts and expressions, one by one.

Do not detain yourself in one fixed role.

There is no need to obliterate your own personality, but be open for self-realization and preserve your inner self.

Always analyze your true feelings and suggestions, and establish them subconsciously in a positive manner.

Think about and picture yourself. Take an interest to motivate yourself to do whatever needs further improvement. Practice repeatedly until the negative forces change into positive and are part of your thinking and actions.

Be organized, experimental, creative.

Conserve time and energy for positive things, but genuinely recognize fatigue.

Take adequate rest.

Use your odd moments productively.

Consolidate your gains with steady work.

Always keep an open mind.

Remember, success is a 50-50 chance, and it is not always permanent; nobody owns it.

But the pleasure while trying to reach success, to struggle for success, and the path to success are yours forever.

Start practicing not reacting to other's emotions or situations. At least immediately or spontaneously, do not react when others start neglecting your presence or when others express some dislike feelings toward you.

Do not react if they don't interact with you, if they don't show you a happy face, if they show you some harshness, if they make some unusual comment.

Don't react with the same feelings in return. Let the flying egos fly freely from them, but don't catch them, and don't take it personally, and don't react with another arrow of ego or false ego.

Until you know their real feelings and the purpose of their behavior, there is no reason to analyze their feelings. Let time decide; by ignoring them, you will do the job of creating no animosity. This saves you a lot of peace of mind. Thinking about other's behaviors and feelings toward you creates unnecessary ripples within yourself. This needs practice each time you come across these situations. Each time, try to react with a pleasurable expression and leave the situation with no negative feeling. Make this a part of your practice. It is a part of the concept of "Prevention is better than treatment."

CHANGES YOU WILL SEE AFTER PRACTICE

No time guidelines work here; remember, Buddha practiced every day until his last minute on earth, despite reaching enlightenment. Soon you will see in yourself a change that stays with. You will be more mindful during every movement. You will enjoy situations and conversations consciously and mindfully, rather than having your mind be somewhere else. You will be more goal oriented and productive. You will deal with your life better and improve your quality of life far better than expectations.

Overall, you will see the change that you always wanted but were not able to achieve in the past. The new self will emerge to stay forever. The change will reflect all aspects of your life. Others will easily see the change and start admiring you.

You will see real joy when you walk your child to school. You will enjoy every movement that you are with your loved ones. Every movement will be a joy-filled memory. You will improve tremendously your patience, your presence of mind, and your feelings of living right now.

Unexpected physical and mental health issues, circumstances, financial problems, and family issues can make you feel like a falling fruit or a free object in the air. They can make you feel so vulnerable that you cannot withstand it and you succumb.

This is the time you need more courage to sustain the gains of all these days and years of practice. Steve Jobs and J. K. Rowling are notable examples of people who won over their own illness; Jobs dealt with physical illness, and Rowling suffered from depression, financial burdens, and insecurity, which can be worse than physical illness.

Live more consciously in those vulnerable times. When we are emotional, we lose logic, and then everything falls apart. It makes us so lonely that despite having hundreds of people around, you are battling with your own thoughts and emotions. For a second, you may become unreasonable and unable to sustain the truth.

In those particularly vulnerable times, goal-oriented practice, sustaining what you did so far, and a positive attitude can take you further in the right direction. It may seem like the end of the line, but you will cross the line so determined with self-respect and dignity of the soul.

This book is a small, sincere effort to stress the importance of practice, practice, and practice. Consistency is the key to the conquest, to bringing your potential out to stay and achieve for you forever, to giving you a really balanced life with quality. Again, practicing without giving up is the key.

Here I presented are some different meditation practices. Whatever works best for you, please take it and practice. If none of these methods work for you, just take home this message: "Practice with diligence and don't give up." Let go of the unpleasant experiences and negative forces within you.

Practice with no denial, repression, regression, or suppression. Don't use any isolation or undoing techniques.

Most of us had positive feelings during childhood. Bring them back to lead your life and to stay with you, to motivate you, to give you more goals, and to make you an achievement-oriented person. Make your success generate more success. Learn to deal with disappointment easily.

Acquire new talents, and get the courage to strive for happiness in a moral line. That comes with effort, practice, power of work, sense of duty, responsibility, and commitment.

There is no end until the end. "No" only means not yet. We will be learning more and more. We are blessed with the opportunity to change, learn, stay happy, and create happiness for our loved ones.

This is nothing but biofeedback and relaxation training, with further scope into higher levels of meditation and empty mindedness. It is particularly useful to redirect our life back to us and helps to control many other medical issues in a better way.

PLAN OF ACTION

Practice is our mode of action. Observe mindfully all the negative and positive forces that are struggling within you.

Understand each other's positive and negative needs, and decide which ones to eliminate. Write down all your negative forces that consistently dominating you, bothering you, and hindering your progress. Let the past events leave with no rumination. Start communicating with your subconscious mind consciously. Again if your mind wanders at the beginning, let it be.

Evaluate yourself from time to time, like you are doing a project. You have to work until consistency prevails in your thoughts. Work toward positive goals only. Habituate your mind with positive thoughts only, and that is the meditation for now. Do not look for enlightenment or empty mindedness.

Your mind will slowly start to settle down and wander less and less, as long as you don't give up your positive thoughts and practice. Make adequate time for relaxation and develop good sleep habits. Stay away from all unhealthy substances. Do not blame anyone, including yourself, for anything. Stop the blame game.

Say "Let it go" each time you start to blame the past or anybody else. Comply with your medical treatment, if any. Look from a broader perspective to see if you need help. In some cases, medication is a part of life, something you need on a daily basis.

Maintain a list of the real issues. From time to time, evaluate the negative forces, if any. Discover the power of consistent practice. Don't give up; let your conscious efforts sync with your subconscious mind.

Slowly, you will see your positive forces appear one by one in your thoughts and actions, in the form of less anger, no grudges, and less envy; you will also see more love and patience, compassion, subdued emotions, rationality, motivation, and a drive to achieve goals and pursue happiness for your loved ones and ultimately yourself.

How to Heal

How can we train our mind to heal and progress in a positive way? How can we achieve our goals while enjoying our life more purposefully?

Enlightenment is a rare phenomenon, but realization is common and within our reach of practice.

Everybody who has a passing thought for changing toward betterment is already touching the realization. To sustain that realization, one only needs sustained practice. To rejoice in the results of realization, one needs to practice further and maintain the practice with moderation.

You are ready for practice. And you need to rebuild a new self, with directions from your old mistakes. The influences that you have may not be with your full consent; they may not be in harmony with your self or with your subconscious thoughts.

All your past experiences, fears, frustrations, false imaginations, and impressions that you have so far are probably keeping you from pursuing change. They are keeping you in the same circle of suffering. You need to generate a powerful force to take you away from those experiences and make a new self, full of motivation and positive, goal-oriented thoughts.

To get to that stage of self-realization, make yourself fully absorbed in your thoughts regarding what you are going to do. No external forces, chance influences, or situations can throw you into the same turmoil again.

Bring your conscious mind and your subconscious mind (the silent watcher) into complete control. Plan each action with harmony; stop your thousands of wrong expressions, millions of bad feelings, and misleading actions, and promote actions instead that will help you. Make all negative thoughts perish, one at a time. Remember, one desire conquered is a hundred desires fulfilled.

One negative thought put to permanent rest will allow room for many positive thoughts. Behave like someone walking in the rain but not getting wet. Be the observer of the events happening without involving yourself.

Everything can be explained and can be done in moderation if the situation requires, but do not indulge, and don't make the same mistakes while you are practicing your realization. Don't desert yourself with self-possession. Changes are gradual and take time and effort. Like we discussed, enlightenment is sudden, but even Buddha practiced for six years before attaining that enlightenment. Instead of realizing that he already possessed it, he was enlightened suddenly that day. But he practiced moderation long before his enlightenment. He did not like the extremes that he was practicing at the beginning of his realization.

But there is nothing wrong in being yourself in any situation and in all circumstances. The whole world is like this, but there is no reason for you to imitate the rest of the world. You can differentiate yourself like butter separates from buttermilk, showing its own state and properties but still staying part of the buttermilk. Feelings of loneliness and separation from loved ones can pop up when you are not doing the same as others, or even if you stay away from your daily worries and circumstances. You may feel uncomfortable; time may feel like it stopped just for you, and a sense of empty loneliness can hold your heart. Withstand them, resist them, and ignore them for a better inner self. Remember J. K. Rowling? Her story is truly inspiring. If she did not resist those movements of despair, depression, and suicidal thoughts, she would not have become what she is today. A moment of self-restraint and motivation for improvement brought her subconscious creativity and imagination, which she was able to capture page by page, bringing Harry Potter to the whole world. She turned all her negatives and self-destructive feelings into positives, with one success that was repeated again and again.

Rowling struggled a lot before she saw success. She endured through struggles to prosperity and happiness. Gandhi said that he did not rejoice only after India won its freedom, but he enjoyed his struggle through all those years of fighting for its freedom.

Rowling's story of personal triumph is more appealing to me than her story of Harry Potter (her success story). But we would not know her without her success through Harry. The struggle she went through was hugely inspiring; she was able to sustain her vision and goal and finish her first Harry Potter novel. While trying to find a publisher, she was rejected many times and became extremely disappointed. And even after her book was accepted by a publisher, she was discouraged when he told her to find a job other than writing. But eventually she proved all of them wrong, and her success saw no end. She is the first novelist to earn billions of dollars.

If Darwin had given up his research and remained depressed, stagnant, and phobic, the world would have missed his extraordinary scientific breakthroughs. If Newton couldn't continue his experiments due to his psychiatric conditions, imagine how much the world would have missed in scientific advancements.

One Unknown source (a poet) said

Life is a drama
A lone voyage
from infancy to fantasy
memories homed in bone
we trudge on and on
each thought an accident
each act a monument.

Still please accept and maintain all good acts and good thoughts to make it more memorable.

SHRED YOUR EGO FOREVER

Discipline your ego. Identify the weak link and act now. Egoism is the worst disease, and the only remedy is identifying it and terminating it. There may be a hidden egoism that is subconsciously making you what you are today. If you are not able to change the way you deal with daily habits; if you cannot change your pattern of behavior with your peers, friends, and higher authorities; if you keep your old habits and easily succumb to peer pressure, then egoism may be the cause.

You may not be able to overcome your own egoism and keep falling into its trap. You may do things that you may regret later just because of that egoism, which can keep you from saying no. Accept it and erase it. Say to yourself, *I am what I am, and I want to be like this with no influences to alter my path toward discipline.* Learn to say no when you need to.

Nobody can help you better than yourself if you fall in the trap of worry's a vicious cycle. Your dear ones, family, parents and friend's only can help to some extent. They can show some sympathy, can help you here and there, now and then or for a while. No body can intrude into your mind and alter it. Medications and therapies all can help to some extent only with your conscious effort added to them. If you don't achieve harmony with your mind and if cannot act in synergy you can't stop worries, rumination. You will sure go back and forth and finally end up where you are now. If you are prepared for a lifetime change and want to sustain the change, your efforts are most beneficial. So again remember,

Twenty years from now you will be more disappointed by the things that you did not do than by the ones you did. So explore, dream, discover the challenge, the joy of growth.—Mark Twain

REMEMBER THIS:

Life is so much to do and not to give up.

Rule your own domain with good control.

You get nothing by sitting in the dark.

You can't see the light while you worry about the dark.

Be happy; live for today because yesterday is over, tomorrow you don't know, but expect tomorrow to be the best.

Remain vigorous all the time.

Tell yourself that searching for a road in the darkness is boring; winning is yin-yang always. But trying is not boring; frustration will make you fall back more.

Do the things that you fear most, one by one, until you feel no fear.

Remember, winning is not permanent; winners can lose too.

But do things the best way.

Note: From time to time, most of us get trapped by depression, anxiety, and attention deficit. So for daily practice, I have included some meditation and diet tips following the conclusion.

Conclusion

OTHER THAN BEING A qualified physician and a neurologist with meditation experience, I asked myself if I was morally qualified to write this book. I faced many negative forces and difficulties in my life, until recently. Each time, the inner core of my positive forces bounced back with resilience, either silencing or neutralizing the negative forces. I always see the positive forces revitalizing me and giving me a newer and better perspective of life. Every time I face a challenge, from necessity, I win over it. Success has no limits, and I counted only from where I started. There is still a lot to see, as we discussed, until the last breath, with 50/50 chances of yin-yang calculations.

I will never stop practicing meditation. I will never stop striving for betterment. I will take it as it comes, and I will stay content during my time on earth. I will act as much as I can with enhanced determination and not give up.

When we were kids, we learned a story about a boy addicted to sweets; the saint Paramahamsa changed his habit. His mother was so worried because her son could not stop eating sugar. And being a devotee of this saint, she took the boy to him, asking him to change her son. After listening to the mother, the saint said to come back in six weeks.

The saint had also been addicted to eating too much cane sugar and sweets, so he felt he was not the right person to advise the boy. During the six weeks, being a saint, he was able to get rid of that habit quickly. He no longer craved sugar and tested himself with sweet temptations around him. Finally, he made sure that he was morally qualified to advise another person on that topic. The story ended well: the boy was influenced by the saint and stopped overeating sweets.

I experienced many temptations and challenges. Difficulties and negative forces engulfed me many times, but self-awareness and consistent practice with determination helped me to bounce back and lead a life with contentment. Nobody is immune to problems, and they will come to all of us until our last breath. I do know the breath holding, agonizing, pinching, achy pain of the soul. This is the most dynamic state, called life. We must face life's difficulties as challenges and as blessings in disguise. We must never give up. I am one among you with a few steps either up or down the road.

Whenever my brother and I used to fight, my mother would punish us by saying, "Both of you, go to that corner and do fifteen minutes of *dhyanam* (Meditation in sanskrit and in my native tongue)." At that age, sitting silently with our eyes closed during the middle of playtime was certainly a punishment. But now we are all trying to change, in order to achieve a better soul. So we all need to embrace that meditation with joy or consider that as an inevitable punishment that we need to go through daily practice, until it becomes an enjoyable tradition and part of our daily routine.

Mere knowledge means nothing. No one is perfect, and we are

not looking for perfectionism either. Only when knowledge meets practice, in the right amount and direction, will effective results come out as a by-product.

Only when two hands clap will there be an actual sound generated. In the same way, we have to merge our knowledge and practice with consistency and replenish ourselves with resilience. Like a river flows to meet the ocean, despite losing its identity and being from that point, let us flow ourselves with our actions to meet that happy soul.

Finally, there is nothing wrong in trying. Life is not for giving up. It is only the beginning. Don't forget the past, but don't hold on to it either. Let the matchless gift of life unravel its ultimate joy with its full potential to reveal. Let us all try to evolve from the conscious and subconscious minds into a superconscious mind, with the constant evolution of perfect thoughts and feelings, hoping to see that through the eyes of our soul.

Learn to say no as needed.

Face the fear from within until you extinguish it.

Practice consistently without giving up.

You are determined now. So make the determination of your goals so that you can achieve them one by one.

There are many definitions of life; I used to think "survival of the fittest" was life, but now I believe facing each situation is the best interpretation of life.

We are responsible for what we are, and whatever we wish ourselves to be, we have the power to make ourselves. If what we are now has been the result of our own past actions,

it certainly follows that whatever we wish to be in the future can be produced by our present actions.—Vivekananda

Before I leave you now with a practice session, I want to make one last request. I hope it will be useful to you.

If nothing seems to be useful and if anything or everything makes no sense in this book, please let it go with no second thought. But please do remember two things:

You are that "Somebody," and only the body that can reveal to yourself.

And also remember, we create ourselves constantly as we go along.

Thank you and good luck to everyone.

DAILY MEDITATION PRACTICE AND DIET TIPS

The following advice is for people with mood disorders, fibromyalgia, depression, anxiety, attention deficit disorder (ADD)/attention deficit hyperactivity disorder (ADHD), and Fibromyalgia

Practice daily without giving up and with the same vigor every day.

Moderation and flexibility are the keys for success in your diet and meditation practices.

Don't ruminate on your illness but steadfastly practice for better results.

Your goal is not worrying, but overcoming the issues.

Mood Disorders

Future for Depression Treatments

Strategic deep brain stimulation of specific brain areas shows some promise for treating resistant depression and also anxiety. Many different pharmaceutical agents are in the pipeline that will soon be available in the market with hopes of greater benefits to treat depression. Addressing the social issues, personal triggers are most relevant to address on a continuous basis. Medications are generally useful for endogenous depression. The lack of neuro hormones like serotonin is also helped by medications that balance those neurotransmitters. Other types of depression need to be addressed with many different modes of therapies.

ADD/ADHD

Adult ADD is very tricky for both the patient and the physician to determine.

It manifests with no hyperactivity, but with a sense of inner restlessness, resulting in frequent job changes, inability to work, disorganized work, poor self-esteem, undertaking of risky behaviors, clashes with authorities, frequent injuries, easy frustration, childish or impulsive behavior, and underachievement.

If you have some of these features, your doctor can evaluate you to eliminate other possible causes

Future Treatments for ADD/ADHD

Although there is no immediate cure, a new understanding of attention deficit disorder and ADHD may be forthcoming. This will ultimately result in improving the personal fulfillment and productivity of people with ADHD. New, nonstimulant medications are on their way, albeit slowly.

Additional research is ongoing to determine the long-term outcome. Studies are being conducted by scientists, and they are beginning to understand the biological nature of attention disorders. New research is allowing them to better understand the inner workings of the brain and to develop new medications and assess new forms of treatment.

Short-Term Prognosis

In about 15 percent of preschool children, there is a particular concern about ADHD, with 5 percent associated with children during the elementary school years.

Long-Term Prognosis

Many children and adolescents do not outgrow ADHD. Associated symptoms and aggressive behavior can carry a poor, long-term prognosis. ADHD may manifest in different ways in adults as compared to children.

Diet

It is not your fault. In most cases, the above issues are familial, endogenous, environmental, or due to circumstances coupled with daily life stressors. Eliminating the coexisting things causing any of these illnesses leaves the diet. Look inward and chart out reasons for your depression, anxiety, or ADD. Write down the times (such as morning or evening) or season (winter or fall) that make you more vulnerable. In some women, the menstrual cycle makes them more vulnerable during that time. Write down all of the situations that make you feel depressed or anxious, or show a lack of motivation, attention, or concentration.

Learn to say no. More than 25 percent of the time, especially in the younger population, that is one of the causes. You do not want to do something, but you cannot say no due to peer pressure or other stressors. That causes inner conflict, restlessness, worry, rumination, and unnecessary, anticipated anxiety and depression. Face the fear from within until you extinguish it, day by day.

Read this Daily

Life is long, and there is much more to do.

Life has endless possibilities and pleasures if you are goal oriented.

Vigor and energy boost the brain function.

Do everything that makes you anxious, one thing at a time.

Think about everything that makes you depressed, one thing at a time.

Face everything that makes you depressed or anxious in a challenging way.

Face the feelings with effort; do not run away from the situation.

As a child, you did the same. You fell and stood up again and again until you learned to walk perfectly.

You can fall and rise from depression and anxiety until you are no longer depressed or anxious.

Life is short. There is only enough time to be happy and to enjoy life's pleasures, so do not lose time to depression and unrest.

Accept depression and anxiety as just another life experience to compare to and learn from it.

Recall some famous people who went through similar stages, like Charles Darwin, Sigmund Freud, and J. K. Rowling.

Stay away from any stimulants or drugs.

Tobacco may make you feel better now, but it will make you feel worse later.

When anticipatory anxiety comes on, tell yourself to postpone it until the actual event occurs.

When anxiety prevails during an event, let it ride with you rather than trying to suppress it. Let it pass through, just as you do not feel the rain when walking in a storm.

Try not to create more ripples in your mind. React to anxiety or depression by just ignoring it.

Meditation is perfect for ADD/ADHD, anxiety, and depression. If you cannot concentrate and meditate on anything in particular, just think of someone you like, or something you like, creating brain activity that takes you away from your current activity.

Take brief naps, if possible, just to calm your brain and mind.

Limit your intake to one or two cups of regular coffee or tea if you cannot stop altogether.

Limit your intake to one beer per day, or alternate one beer and an equivalent alcoholic beverage if you cannot stay away from it completely. You should stay far away from any mind-altering drugs, alcohol, and nonprescription stimulants.

Adult ADD/ADHD causes a lot of self-questioning. With biofeedback, try to speak only as needed. You can get the same results from therapy and psychological counseling.

People with depression, anxiety, or ADD can develop sleep issues and body aches, which can lead to fibromyalgia, migraines, chronic sleep difficulties, insomnia, and fits.

Your goal is to avoid those problems. You want to be productive and enjoy the pleasures of life.

Do not skip doses of your prescription medicines or counseling appointments.

Self-counseling is studying yourself and taking away the mental blocks and obstacles that cause or provoke your depression, anxiety, or ADD; it can help to eliminate them effectively.

Despite good potential, a lot of patients with ADD/ADHD, anxiety, or depression lose opportunities. They change jobs frequently, do not reach their potential, and have frequent trouble with higher authorities at their workplace.

Use self-counseling and self-talk in situations where you need them; become indispensable by showing your talent and skills.

A positive approach can lead to progress at work. Day by day, you will see good results at work, at home, and personally.

Diet

Take any medication that has been prescribed regularly.

Maintain regular hours for sleep. Get enough sleep, at least seven to eight hours each night (if you are not a short sleeper).

Exercise at least twenty to thirty minutes on most days of the week.

Do meditation to calm your mind. Use deep-breathing techniques to help with anxiety and anger.

Relaxation training and meditation will help to increase focus and concentration, as well as reduce distractions.

Eliminate items from your diet that you think are causing difficulties with attention, anger, and focus.

Experiment with foods that help to soothe your mind and adhere to them in a regular fashion.

Avoid any foods or additives you are allergic to. You will know only by trying them. Avoid artificial colors, especially red and yellow.

Avoid food additives such as aspartame, monosodium glutamate (MSG), and nitrites. Some studies have linked hyperactivity to the intake of the preservative sodium benzoate.

Some people become hyperactive after eating candy or other sugary foods.

Caffeine

Some studies have shown that small amounts of caffeine may help with some ADHD symptoms. However, the side effects of caffeine may outweigh any potential benefit. Avoid caffeine as much as possible. Having small amounts, especially in the morning and afternoon, is okay.

Make any dietary changes slowly over time, but eliminate the foods that are causing ADD/ADHD symptoms immediately.

Overall

Eat a high protein diet that includes beans, eggs, meat, fish, and nuts. Eat less sugar and fewer simple carbohydrates such as candy, corn syrup, honey, products made from white flour, white rice, and potatoes. Eat more vegetables and fruits, including oranges, citrus, pears, apples, and kiwis.

ADD/Depression/Anxiety Meditation

Try meditation in the usual sitting position if possible. Do it as long as you can, for at least half an hour to one hour per day. Limit meditation to once or twice a day. Morning is the best time for meditation. Sleep time meditation as the second session is useful. The bedtime meditation can be done in sleeping posture. It is okay to call asleep while doing meditation.

Depression

Tell yourself:

"Nobody is the winner."

"It is a 50/50 chance."

"Nobody is a loser."

If you think only about the dark, you cannot appreciate the light.

It is too boring to walk in the dark.

Diet

Make sure your medications are helping, and take them regularly.

Follow a good diet program.

Look good to yourself. It makes a lot of difference in your self-esteem.

When you look in the mirror, you should be asking yourself what is lacking to make you feel depressed. This means your appearance brings more self-esteem and motivation. Stand in front of the mirror alone, calm and quiet, and have a brief conversation with yourself. It is like exploring yourself.

Eat right and eat well. Maintain excellent table manners, especially while dining with others or family members.

Choose your foods carefully.

Even though there is no specific diet plan for depression, eat regularly, without skipping meals and without overeating.

Avoid snacks and drinking sodas, which are quite often consumed while depressed along with sitting on the couch. Anorexia is also common.

Good Foods

Eat a normal range of proteins, carbohydrates, and fats.

Avoid high-protein and high-calorie food.

Avoid all stimulants other than prescription medications, including coffee, not drinking it more than twice a day.

Expose yourself to sunlight every day for thirty minutes to an hour.

Take vitamin D and a multivitamin daily, as needed.

Beans and legumes, lean meat like chicken and turkey, low-fat dairy products, nuts, and seeds are good. Seafood and whole grains should be eaten daily.

Eat whatever you feel like on festive occasions and at parties. Stay away from large quantities or habitual use of alcohol.

Anxiety Diet

Work on your anticipatory anxiety first.

Practice biofeedback and meditation daily.

Avoid coffee, alcohol, and stimulants.

A slightly higher protein diet on a daily basis is good.

Avoid pure sugars and snacks.

Eat more fruits.

If you have IBS or lack of sleep because of your anxiety, drink more fluids, but avoid sodas and diet drinks.

Pay attention to food sensitivities.

Try to eat healthy, balanced meals.

Try to avoid fried foods; choose fruits like peaches or berries or nuts like almonds instead.

Fibromyalgia

Follow your doctor's advice and take your medications regularly.

Do not give up on medications by trying them for a short while or small, initial doses.

A lot of medications for fibromyalgia need to be taken for a longer period at optimal doses before concluding that a particular medication is not for you.

Diet

Think of fibromyalgia as a non-life-threatening illness. It will not do harm to any of your vital organs.

It does not damage your heart, brain, kidneys, or any other vital organs.

It is a chronic and painful illness and can be debilitating to muscles and the fascia.

Knowing this, you may come to the conclusion that it is a blessing compared cancer and other serious illnesses.

Maintain a strict daily routine. Good sleep is highly beneficial. Go to bed at regularly scheduled times, preferably around 10:30 p.m., and wake up around 6:30 a.m.

Before getting up, stay in bed for ten minutes to meditate, or sit up quietly.

Afterward, get up out of the bed and stretch your spine and all of your muscles: neck, hips, shoulders, elbows, and arms.

Walk from room to room, preferably on carpet, on toes and heels, doing this twice.

Drink a large bottle of water or grape or orange juice.

Try not to drink coffee, soda, caffeinated beverages, or alcohol.

Take a good hot shower.

Stretch all your muscles before you put on your clothes.

Stretch your fingers and wrists and elbow joints. Follow simple stretching exercises.

Now get ready and go to your work as vigorously as possible after a good breakfast.

While at work, try to stretch all your muscles up to three times a day.

Try to take a nap, just for ten minutes during midday. You need not go into a deep sleep, just try to relax and forget about the world, your surroundings, and yourself. Say to yourself that you are not there.

Take one day at a time to treat your fibromyalgia.

Stretching never hurts.

Diet

Eat regularly and moderately in variety, quality, and quantity.

Choose foods that you tolerate well.

Avoid high sugars, caffeinated sodas, diet colas, and some vegetables like tomatoes, broccoli, cabbage, and cauliflower.

Avoid caffeine, artificial sweeteners, and MSG.

Drink plenty of fluids, eat whole grains as tolerated, and balanced food with meat, protein, fish, egg whites, and cereals.

If you are overweight, try to cut down on fatty foods.

If you tolerate it, taking a daily vitamin with minerals is good.

Get exposure to enough sunlight every afternoon. Avoid evening sun.

Get exposure to the morning sun for half an hour to one hour. Melatonin aids in better sleep. If you sleep better, 50 percent of your pain will be gone the next day. Do meditation if possible in the afternoon or evening.

Use morning time for stretching exercises.

Maintain daily standard sleep times.

Do not sleep at odd times.

If you take a brief nap, limit it to half an hour to forty-five minutes only.

Prefer standard meditation practice, unless you cannot sit up.

If possible, do this at least two or three times per day.

Note

PEOPLE WITH NEUROLOGICAL PROBLEMS like traumatic brain injury, postconcussion syndrome, transient ischemic attack (TIA or stroke), Alzheimer's disease, dementia, memory problems, multiple sclerosis, chronic dizziness, Parkinson's disease, migraines and other headaches, epilepsy, and seizures, please refer to the separate title " Replenish" where individual diet and meditation practice tips are designed to fit the specific disease states and to improve the recovery chances.

End Note

_____

THIS "REVEAL" IS A small but sincere effort to stress the importance of practice, practice, practice (consistency is the key to success) to show our potential, to continue to achieve forever, and to give us a very balanced life.

Reveal: Let It Go is about knowing our shortcomings and accepting them by creating harmony between the conscious and subconscious minds. By doing so with consistent practice, we can overcome all our difficulties and reach our potential.

It is about proving that when we consistently practice the basic concepts of "Don't give up" and "Let it go" with "moderation in practice," we will reach our goals far more than expected.

Famous people also suffer from family and personal tragedies; they are not immune to medical, psychiatric, or neurological disorders. They may have tried several ways of practical life, experimental, innovative foods, and dietary habits. Despite their shortcomings, they have achieved distinction and fame for themselves and have contributed to society by not giving up their goals. Whatever happened in their lives, they were persistent and did not deviate from their goals. They set goals that were high to reach and did not deviate from them despite their personal shortcomings.

Gandhi, Buddha, Darwin, Newton, and Steve Jobs are famous examples. Their primary goal was to reach their target. J. K. Rowling, the author of *Harry Potter,* is one living legend, a case of fighting financial crises, personal loss, and depression. She still used her excellent imagination and contributed her brilliant writings to the world.

Finally, *Reveal: Let It Go* is about rebuilding our soul by continuously learning and improving our brain and our mind's capabilities, with the help of consistent but moderate meditation practice and ideal dietary practices.

Index